SUNSHINE ON THE PRAIRIE

Cynthia Ann Parker, shown nursing her infant daughter, Prairie Flower. This is the only known photograph of Cynthia Ann.

— Courtesy Western History Collections, University of Oklahoma Library

THE STORY OF
CYNTHIA ANN PARKER
SUNSHINE
ON THE
PRAIRIE

By

JACK C. RAMSAY, JR.

EAKIN PRESS ✺ Fort Worth, Texas
www.EakinPress.com

This work is dedicated to
KARIN KINSEY RAMSAY,
a seventh-generation Texan
whose ancestors were part of the Parker migration.
This story could not have been told
without her ability as a researcher and
an interviewer
and her inspiring encouragement.

Quanah Parker in ceremonial attire.
— Courtesy Western History Collections, University of Oklahoma Library

Contents

Quanah Parker, famous son of Cynthia Ann, later in life.
— Courtesy Western History Collections, University of Oklahoma Library

Preface

The story of Cynthia Ann Parker has long been a part of the legend of the western frontier. Unlike many legends, however, it is a tale which is based solidly on fact.

The account of a young girl, whisked away from her natal family in a violent raid on white settlement, who eventually became the mate of a dreaded Comanche war chief, has about it the pathos and the dramatic impact which has long excited the imagination.

It has been the subject of theatrical productions, poetry, and paperback novels.

As a youth growing up in Texas, the author had heard the story. For a time he lived in the area of West Texas where the final acts of the Parker drama were played out as the last of the Comanche remnant took refuge from the relentless efforts of the military to bring about their destruction.

In later years he came across a variety of references to the capture and recapture of Cynthia Ann and the events which led her son, Quanah, to become the last chief of the Comanches. While engaged in another research project, he located a little-known manuscript which proved to be the most accurate of the eyewitness accounts of the raid on Fort Parker. This led to an investigation into a wide range of other information related to facts about the life of the Parker captive.

Archival records and materials from Anglo sources, however, provided only a limited, and, in many ways, a biased account. Too much of the history of the Southwest has been written entirely from the viewpoint of the white frontiersman who viewed the Native Americans merely as an impediment to white settlement.

From the author's own family connections he was able to secure access to materials which gave additional clues to the life of Cynthia Ann. His wife, Karin, provided assistance in research. A descendant of Silas Bates, she had a unique interest in the story, for it was Bates who, according to family tradition, rescued Cynthia Ann's younger sister and later married her. An effective interviewer, Karin was able to secure a vast amount of data directly from Comanche Parker descendants.

The search for information led to a wide variety of sources. The trail for the researchers wound all of the way from the South Plains, through the gates of Fort Sill, across the vast expanses of reservation land, to the holdings of area and state libraries, and eventually to the National Archives in Washington, D.C.

From the accumulated data, it soon became apparent that the capture of Cynthia Ann was not a singular action which was totally unrelated to the history of the Southwest. The events revolving around the raid were but an initial stage of the long and bitter contest for the control of the South Plains. This was a war which would end only when the son of the captured maiden finally led a battered remnant toward peace and demanded from his conquerors decent treatment for the Indian.

When all of the facts emerged, the true story became far more intriguing than fantastic.

This is one of the genuine sagas of the American West.

It is the saga of Cynthia Ann Parker.

"Danger gleams like sunshine
in the eyes of the brave . . ."
— Euripides

Wanda Parker, daughter of Quanah Parker and granddaughter of Cynthia Ann, was about seventeen years old when this picture was taken around 1898.

— From original photo owned by Jake "Tee-cau-lee-skee" Proctor, Sunset Beach, California.

Dawn came early to the Texas prairie.

The first light of the sun fell obliquely across the land beneath a crystal clear sky. The unique serenity which follows sunrise was interrupted only by the sounds of settlers busy with morning chores at Parker's Fort.

Women were at work within the frontier enclosure. The occasional clatter of utensils gently transcended the muted voices of those engaged in the tasks of early morning.

Smoke rose in lazy spirals above cooking fires. There was no wind at the hour, only a peaceful calm.

Outside the fort, a dog barked.[1] No other sound gave hint of potential danger.

Most of the men had left the cabins near the walls of the enclosure to tend crops which had been planted a mile or more away. Their tasks were those which were necessary for survival.

Life had not been easy for these pioneers who had dared ven-

1

ture beyond the outer fringe of white settlement.

Severe weather had plagued their efforts from the beginning of their migration to the frontier. Their early attempts at cultivation had resulted in scant harvests, but now their years of toil were about to produce results. Careful planting and good rains earlier in the season gave promise of ample crops. This would be the best harvest they had seen since their arrival in Texas.

No longer were they wagon-train wanderers.

Like the plants in the nearby fields, they had put down roots.

Suitable cabins had been built. Logs firmly planted in the ground surrounded their living area to provide what they thought would be protection against hostile attack.

7:00 A.M.

Daylight now flooded the surrounding prairie.

As the early morning sunshine of May called forth moisture from the soil, the fields near the fort began to possess a succulent vitality. The pungent aroma of verdant greenery brought reassurance to those who had survived a long and difficult winter.

But this was not the only hopeful sign for these newcomers to Texas. There was encouraging news from the settlements to the east.

Santa Anna's army, which had marched into the province from south of the Rio Grande early in the year, had been turned back at San Jacinto. Those who had fled, fearful of the power of the invader, were making plans to return; those who had dared to stay took encouragement from the fact that Texas was no longer under siege.

The mellowness of the morning sun helped erase all recollection of past hardships. This was no time for fear: even the most cautious could be lulled into a sense of careless relaxation.

8:00 A.M.[2]

Suddenly, there was the sound of hoofbeats.

Within moments the resounding, rhythmic noise of a large group of riders materialized into a band of Indian warriors. The unannounced visitors reined in just beyond the bounds of the settlement.

Several of the fort's inhabitants peered from behind the protection of their log-palisaded walls. The main gate had been left open, probably by the men who had gone to the fields before daybreak.

The mien of the visitors, however, seemed to show no immediate cause for alarm.

The gate remained open.

Benjamin Parker, one of several brothers who had been a part of this migration to the frontier, walked cautiously out to greet the Indian band in an effort to show that the settlers felt no hostility toward the natives of the area. He was informed that the visitors were seeking water and a place to camp. That was no problem: there were well-watered campsites in the area.

But they also wanted food.

He returned to the fort to discuss the possibility of sharing with their unexpected guests the meager supplies of beef which the settlers had on hand. He conferred briefly with his father, John Parker, an aging veteran of the American Revolution, and the handful of men who were still present in the fort.

There was little to be discussed. Food had been scarce from the beginning of their migration.

A satisfactory crop was yet to be harvested.

8:15 A.M.

Benjamin Parker emerged from the protection of the settlement enclosure empty-handed.

Suddenly, the peaceful scene erupted into violence. He was surrounded and killed.

"I saw them gathering around Uncle Benjamin . . . [into whom] I saw them stabbing their spears," Rachel Plummer, one of the young women inside the fort, later recalled.[3]

Within moments, the marauders swarmed into the fort.

Since most of the males of the settlement were in the fields some distance away, there were only a few potential defenders present to stem the tide of invasion. Whatever efforts they made to protect themselves and the women and children proved to be futile. The men were immediately overwhelmed by their attackers.

They were quickly downed. Spears were driven into their bodies. A bloody ritual followed: they were scalped, and, as a final insult to their manhood, their genitals were ripped from their bodies as they died in agony.[4]

The attackers turned their attention to the terrified female members of the settlement.

Rachel Plummer recalled that one of the marauders knocked her down, tore her infant son from her arms, and dragged her to the center of the fort.

"I swooned away, how long I know not."[5]

One of the older women, Granny Duty, was attacked. She offered as much resistance as any of the men. She was stripped naked, pinned to the ground with a spear, and gang raped. Other women in the enclosure were rounded up and subjected to similar abuse.[6]

James W. Parker, the father of Rachel Plummer, was among those working in the fields when the raid began.[7] He later reported the situation succinctly: "Elder John Parker, a Revolutionary Soldier of the U.S. Army, Benjamin Parker and Silas M. Parker, Samuel Frost, and Robert B. Frost was [sic] killed."[8]

Parker placed the attacking force at "some 100," whom he said had approached the fort "under a white flag."[9]

The band of Indians, a group of Comanches who had been joined by some Kiowas and possibly a few Wichitas and Caddoans, proceeded to take what they wanted, including women and children. The raiders were not an organized war party with a singular goal. Instead they were simply a collection of young warriors bent on unleashing their frustrations on any group of whites they found encroaching upon the territory which had long been the domain of the Indian. They believed they were protecting an area which was rightfully a part of their heritage.[10]

Since the winter of 1835–1836 had been a severe one,[11] this band of roving braves had taken to the trail with the coming of spring. They sought food, goods which might have some value for their several tribes, and hostages who could be exchanged for silver.

The Indian was aware that the numbers of Anglo settlers were rapidly growing. The massacre and the mutilation of the men and the sexual attacks on the women were declarations that the increase of white settlement both by migration and birth must be stopped.

8:30 A.M.

The marauders began a search for valuable items which could be taken from the fort. Having sated their appetite for violence, they seemed particularly interested in finding supplies of medicine.

Rachel Plummer later said that her mistreatment continued for half an hour, during which time she saw "bloody scalps" which had been taken from the men of the fort.[12] By this time she had sufficiently recovered from her fainting spell to be aware of her circumstances. When she was later asked by her tormentors about the yellow powder they had found in the fort, she encouraged them to paint themselves with the substance. It was "pulverized arsenic," which she insisted they should mix with their own saliva. This, she recalled with gleeful satisfaction, "did not fail to kill them."[13]

It is possible that her subtle retaliation resulted in more deaths than that of the number of the fort's defenders who died in the initial attack.

Whatever goods the invaders could not easily carry away, they destroyed, cutting open feather beds and scattering supplies that had no value to them.[14]

Lucy Parker, whose husband Silas was one of the first to lose his life, fled from the scene with her four children. Sarah Nixon escaped through the fort's back entrance and ran desperately toward those who were working the crops in the fields.[15]

8:45 A.M.

Once aware that their settlement was under siege, the men in the fields grabbed their hoes and implements and started back to the fort. Silas Bates, David and Evan Faulkenberry, L. D. Nixon, J. W. Parker, and the others working the crops rushed toward the scene. Upon arriving at the site of the massacre, they were able to dampen the ardor of the remaining attackers, who had broken into small groups of marauders seeking trophies of their raid.[16]

Recalling her ordeal, Rachel Plummer remembered hearing "Uncle Silas shout a most triumphant huzza as tho' he had thousands to back him."[17]

By this time the raiders were engaged in rounding up potential hostages. One group of Comanches overtook Lucy Parker and her children in their flight from the fort, forced the older son and daughter onto horses behind the warriors, and would have taken the others had they not been discouraged by the arrival of the Bates-Faulkenberry party.[18]

9:00 A.M.

The raiders began a rapid retreat.

Aware that retaliation was possible and not knowing when settler reinforcements might arrive, the Indians headed northward. They took with them the loot they had gathered and five hostages: the two Parker children, two young women, and an infant.

The Anglo survivors of the raid left soon afterwards. Fearful that such a large band of Indians might stay in the area and continue to bring destruction and death, the remaining settlers sought refuge in a nearby forest of trees and thick underbrush.

An eyewitness account described their plight: "James W. Parker conducted a company of eighteen persons principally bare footed women and children six days and nites through the woods with nothing to eat but thimer skunks."[19] In order to make very clear what their diet was during those days of flight, Parker, who wrote the account himself, added after the word "skunks" the term "polecats."[20]

When at last the fugitives cautiously returned to their settlement to seek supplies of food which had been hidden in the fort, they found themselves faced with the difficult task of burying the decomposing bodies of the men who had been scalped and mutilated. There was one body they did not have to bury: that was the still living, ghostlike form of Granny Duty. She had survived her ordeal. She emerged from one of the cabins badly wounded, but very much alive.[21]

10:00 A.M.

By midmorning the raiders were a dozen or more miles north of the settlement. They had no intention of staying in the area. They rode rapidly along the unmarked trail toward the Red River. Their destination was the territory north of the river in which the Indian believed himself to be secure from counterattack.

J. W. Parker's account listed the five whites, who, by this time, were well on their way into captivity: "Elizabeth Kellog (widow), Rachel Plummer and her infant child James, Sinthy Ann *[sic]* and John Parker, children of Silas M. Parker."[22]

Elizabeth Kellog was a relative of the Parkers by marriage and Rachel Plummer was James Parker's daughter. John Parker was a boy of six years and his sister, Cynthia Ann, was nine.

3:00 P.M.

The fast-moving Comanche ponies had carried the captors and the captives beyond the reach of potential pursuers by midafternoon.

Although confident they had outdistanced anyone who would dare follow them, the riders did not pause in their trek toward Indian territory.

As the intense heat of late May bore down upon the prairie, the two women and three children continued their forced journey into the unknown.

7:00 P.M.

Even with the approach of darkness, the raiders did not stop. Their ponies were surefooted. The Indians continued to ride into the night, traveling as rapidly as their mounts could carry them.

12:00 A.M.

By midnight the hostages found themselves bound with raw-hide thongs and lying on the ground in the midst of an Indian encampment. They had been carried more than a normal day's ride away from the site of Fort Parker.

Rachel Plummer described her plight: she was painfully tied on her first night of captivity after which her captors "turned me on my face" and began "dancing around the scalps."[23]

The other captives lay nearby.

None knew what fate awaited them.

All of the captives would survive their ordeal. Four of the five hostages would be returned to their homes.

Only one would not: the nine-year-old daughter of the slain Silas Parker and his wife Lucy.

Her name was Cynthia Ann.

II.

A Promised Land

The Parker migration had arrived in the Mexican province of Texas early in the year 1834.

The pioneering party had come by caravan following the Mississippi River southward from Illinois. During the fall of 1833 they made their way down the trail which followed the valley of the river to north central Louisiana, where they camped for two months in Claiborne Parish. From there they turned their wagons to the west and crossed the Sabine River at Logansport, Louisiana.[1]

Although this group of settlers had left behind them the heavy snows of Illinois, there was still bitter cold in the air as they arrived in Texas. It was as though they had brought a portion of their northern climate with them. This was a winter which would be remembered in later times as one of extreme inclemency,[2] a fact which added to their difficulties as they continued their trek toward the land they had been told would be ideal for settlement.

The Conestoga wagon, the basic mode of transportation for the westward moving pioneer of the North American continent, could make steady progress on the open prairie and was capable of moving with ease along hardened trails. River crossings, however, presented a peculiar difficulty for these vehicles with their high rear wheels some six feet in diameter guided by smaller wheels near the forward portion of the long, heavily constructed chassis. Goods and passengers generally had to be unloaded to avoid miring in water-laden sands. The wagons then had to be carefully guided across the stream and then reloaded before forward progress could continue. The route this group had chosen had taken them across several streams which had included the Red River.

The Sabine was their last river to cross, a crossing which took place soon after the first day of the year. By January 20, they had moved nearly one hundred miles into the center of white settlement in north central Texas.[3] There they began the difficult task of building dwellings which would make it possible to survive the remainder of the winter.

Led by the oldest son of John Parker, Daniel, the party had left Illinois in the late summer of 1833.[4] During their sojourn in northern Louisiana they had added members to their entourage. Family records indicate that several persons joined the caravan under the influence of Daniel Parker, who conceived of the journey to Texas as a religious pilgrimage. He had led his followers to the Southwest seeking not only land for cultivation and sites for homes, as did most pioneers, but for another purpose: he and his adherents had come to Texas with the avowed intention of finding a place to practice a unique form of religious belief. These were pilgrims seeking a promised land.

Daniel had made a trip to Texas in the spring of 1833.[5] Accompanied by his brother James, the two had sought both a site for settlement and a place to organize a Predestinarian Baptist Church that would adhere to the Two-Seeds-in-the-Spirit doctrine for which Daniel was famous.[6]

A dozen years earlier, he had broken with the majority of his fellow Baptists over the issue of the validity of foreign missions. In 1824 he had written a twenty-eight-page pamphlet entitled "A Public Address to the Baptist Society," in which he vigorously opposed sending missionaries to non-Christian lands. Two additional pamphlets were published in 1827 by Parker, who by this time had gained widespread attention for his theological position.

He continued his doctrinal disputes in publications and religious periodicals for the next several years. Before his departure for the Texas frontier, he intermingled his religious disputations with his political efforts as he sought a place in the House of Representatives in Washington.[7]

As the leader of this pilgrim band, he was not only a writer of national renown, but a fiery declaimer of his faith.

Daniel Parker, according to one source, had "acquired wide celebrity as a pulpit orator and expounder of his eccentric views . . . [however, he] was a man of splendid intellect."[8] Another estimate of him declared he was "one of the ablest men in Illinois in his time . . . [but he was] a scourge to the church."[9]

The Parkers were among those who had continued to move westward with the frontier. John Parker, the family patriarch, had settled in Culpepper County, Virginia, where Daniel was born. From there the Parkers trekked to Georgia and established a farm on the Savannah River. The next stop westward was Tennessee.[10]

The two oldest sons of the family, Daniel and Isaac, joined the militia during the War of 1812 and fought in the Battle of Horseshoe Bend against Creek Indians who were believed to have been incited by the British. The military operation was led by Andrew Jackson.

Daniel Parker served as paymaster for Jackson's army during the Indian conflict. He became a strong admirer of the future president and later declared the general to be "a fine fellow [who] has no disposition to interfere with duties which do not dissolve upon him . . . He is a very polished courtly man."[11] A fellow Tennessean named Sam Houston was also involved in the encounter.[12]

The family continued to move with the frontier, following the Cumberland River, crossing the Ohio, then along that river to the Wabash to settle in Crawford County, Illinois. One chronicler of the Parker family recorded that John Parker had acquired the title Elder John as a leader in the Primitive Baptist Church and that he "conducted . . . church services wherever they had a small band of believers . . ."[13]

A total of six sons were born to the Parkers: Daniel, Isaac, John, James, Silas, and Benjamin. By the time the family settled in Illinois, all were married except the youngest, Benjamin. It was Silas who, during the family's sojourn in Crawford County, married Lucy Duty. In 1827 they became the parents of a daughter, Cynthia Ann.[14]

By this time, Daniel, as the oldest son, had assumed a position of leadership for the family. He had already established a reputation as a forceful pulpit orator and was noted for working all day on his farm and then walking as much as twenty miles to fulfill a preaching appointment.[15]

In 1822 he was elected a state senator of Illinois and took a vigorous stand against slavery. However, he failed to be reelected in 1826 and was later unsuccessful as a candidate for the United States House of Representatives.[16]

There was increasing excitement about the fact that land was available in Texas. Glowing accounts were being written about the province claimed by Mexico but now being settled by Anglo pioneers. It was described as "a land of promise and fruition."[17]

Daniel was determined to spy out this new promised land. Taking his brother James with him, he journeyed to Texas, and early in 1833, applied for a land grant.[18] The two brothers were encouraged by what they saw. One major problem, however, existed: there was a legal prohibition against the establishment of any religious congregation other than one of the Roman Catholic faith.

This was no serious impediment for the resourceful Parkers. Daniel and James returned to Illinois, made their report that they had found Texas to be a land of milk and honey, and, as a part of their preparations to transport the Parker family to the new land of promise, solemnly constituted themselves as a church outside of Mexican-controlled territory. Then they prepared to move as a congregation by wagon train to Texas. One report stated that they departed from Illinois with "about twenty-five wagons, mostly ox drawn."[19]

Formally organized July 26, 1833, in Illinois, the church was appropriately called "The Pilgrim Primitive Baptist Church."[20]

In January 1834, eleven members of the Parker clan established the previously organized church on the soil of their new land and solemnly recorded a gathering in the home of Daniel Parker.[21] A replica of the original log building now stands on a site a few miles from Palestine, Texas, with a marker declaring this to be the "oldest Protestant church in Texas."[22]

The type of religion which Daniel Parker and his successors proclaimed is indicated in an extant document which described a brush arbor meeting held in Central Texas a few years after the establishment of the Pilgrim Church. The preacher, a descendant of Daniel, who considered himself "half Parker," was twice interrupted by a mischievous boy. He stopped in the middle of a sentence, left the pulpit, and proceeded to beat the lad to his knees. On returning to the podium he commented that "if I had been all Parker, I guess I would have killed that boy," and then he continued preaching without forgetting the exact phrase upon which he had stopped.[23]

After surviving the winter of 1834 in East Texas, the party divided. Silas Parker was among those members of the family who moved toward the Southwest, crossing the Trinity River to the head of the Navasota where a settlement was established in Limestone County near the present-day town of Groesbeck. Eight or nine families were in this band of adventurers which included Grandfather John, the family patriarch who, in his lifetime, had moved over 3,000 miles on foot and horseback. More than two dozen persons were a part of this group which dared venture beyond the outer fringe of the frontier. They ranged in ages from white-haired grandparents to unweaned infants.[24]

Once again severe weather conditions made an impact upon the existence of these pioneers. Extant records indicate that this was a period of continuing inclemency. Violent winter storms swept across the plains and penetrated deep into the area where the Parkers were seeking to build a settlement. Food supplies were sparse and the shelter they were able to build initially was barely adequate. Not only did this scarcity cause hardship for the white settlers, but it meant roving tribes of Indians to the west would be an even greater threat for the Anglo newcomers.[25]

In spite of bitter cold and blustery northers, the Parkers went to work at the task of settlement. Trees were chopped from nearby stands of timber. These were carefully fashioned into logs for cabins to provide some protection from the weather. Land was cleared for cultivation in the hope that a crop could be planted with the coming of spring.

Food and shelter, however, were not their only concerns. Realizing they were in territory subject to Indian raids, a sturdy fort of upright timber was built as security against hostile attack. A stockade was constructed, according to Parker family sources, which was ten or twelve feet high. Timbers were placed so closely together that an attacker could not penetrate the outer walls or easily set fire to the inner structures of the fort. The entire enclosure was a rectangle measuring 234 feet in length and about 200 feet in width. Blockhouses were erected at the corners, providing effective defensive firepower against marauders.[26]

The fortification was a substantial one which could have withstood an attack and a long siege when adequately defended. The very erection of such an edifice was a declaration that the Parkers had come to stay and were determined to tame their portion of the frontier.

III.

The Forty Year War

The Texas which the Parkers had entered in 1834 was a land in revolution.

Soon after Mexico had severed its ties with Spain, the newly declared republic threw open the doors of the province north of the Rio Grande to Anglo settlement. Largely at the urging of Moses Austin, an American who had declared himself a citizen of Mexico, a liberal colonization law was passed early in 1823. The door remained open to settlers from the north and east for the remainder of the decade.

Under the leadership of Moses' son, Stephen F. Austin, Anglo settlers came into the Mexican province in large numbers during the final years of the decade. However, these newcomers to Texas soon found themselves to be aliens in a legal and cultural system which they little understood. Resentment quickly developed over laws which were administered from outside of the province by a governmental system in which they had no representation.

In 1830 the central authorities of Mexico became alarmed over the success of the settlement program which had been in place for

15

half a dozen years. Responding to internal political pressures, the Mexican government suddenly reversed the policy of colonization. A law was passed in Mexico City which cut off immigration and threatened to put an end to the continued development of Texas.

Initially, the influx of settlers into Mexico's northernmost province had been both sanctioned and encouraged by the nation's political leadership. They had been confident that the newcomers would bring economic growth to the area, producing tariffs which would enrich the coffers of the central government. In addition, white settlement in Texas would serve as an effective buffer against the natives of the area. For centuries nomadic bands of Indians had dominated the Southwest. Hostile raids by Comanches and Apaches upon the Mexican interior had occurred on occasion. By the end of the decade, however, authorities in Mexico began to wonder if the continuing influx of North Americans into the province might not be more of a threat to the security of Mexico than that of the Indians of the High Plains.

The cessation of immigration was not the only problem for the Anglos who had come to Texas. Those who had legally entered the area soon found themselves in conflict with the authorities over the questions of land titles and the sporadic and often uneven collection of tariffs.

In 1832 Stephen F. Austin, who had been responsible for bringing the first immigrants into the province, called for a convention in an effort to find solutions to the problems of the settlers. At this gathering, which he personally led, recommendations were drawn up which were to be forwarded to governmental authorities. His efforts, however, met with an immediate rebuff. Since the conference had not been authorized by Mexican officialdom, the entire proceedings were suspect and the convention was declared to be illegal.

Austin was a man of determination. He was not willing to give up his attempt at a peaceful solution to the problems of the colonists. In 1833 he called for another assembly, this time with some degree of official acquiescence. At this second gathering, the delegates drew up a statement of grievances. Austin was one of three commissioners selected to present the Texas petitions directly to the government in Mexico City. It was only Austin, however, who dared make the journey to the seat of government to lay the case of the colonists before the national authorities. He initially received a hearing in Mexico, but before he could return home, the political climate in the Mexican capital changed. He was arrested, jailed, and held in a Mexican prison until the end of 1834.

When the news of Austin's imprisonment reached the colonists, distrust turned to anger. Most were now convinced that statesmanship and diplomacy were useless. The revolutionary fervor which had been increasing in intensity since the beginning of the decade reached new heights.

Many of the colonists were ready to fight.

During the summer of 1835, settlers began to congregate throughout the province. In these gatherings armed rebellion was openly proclaimed as the only solution to the problems of the Texans. As the heat of the summer increased, so did the fervor of impromptu orators. In one place after another there were those who declaimed "publicly in favor of independence."[1]

Soon after Fort Parker had been built, Daniel Parker left the frontier to join the effort to throw off the yoke of the Mexican control of Texas. Doubtless the legal strictures against the practice of his religion played a significant part in his decision to join the battle for the independence of Texas.

Although he was a man who was accustomed to bearing arms, he had an even more powerful weapon for furthering the cause of revolution in his adopted land. He became an orator of the independence movement. Traveling from campfire to campfire, he urged his fellow settlers to arm themselves for a contest to free Texas from the control of the government in Mexico City.

One account indicated Daniel Parker was present when the Texans camped on the banks of Salado Creek twelve miles east of San Antonio in the fall of 1835. He was among those who "orated the troops" before the battle which drove a Mexican garrison from the city.[2]

In December an army of 700 Texans, spurred on by the enthusiasm of declaimers like Parker, stormed San Antonio. After several days of house-to-house fighting, the Mexican commandant, Gen. Martín Perfecto de Cos, raised a white flag, and, after agreeing to leave Texas, marched his troops back to Mexico.

There were many who believed this initial victory meant the end of both military and economic oppression for Texas. The members of the militia which had taken San Antonio returned to their homes.

Within weeks, however, the enemy recrossed the Rio Grande.

Early in 1836, Gen. Antonio López de Santa Anna moved a sizable army northward from Mexico and retook San Antonio. There, after a determined siege, he destroyed a garrison of Texans who had sought to impede his progress by barricading themselves in an abandoned mission known as the Alamo. By the end of March, his troops had gunned down the captured remnants of another band of revolutionists near Goliad.

Santa Anna was in complete control of the southern half of Texas.

Family after family picked up their belongings and left for the safety of the United States. "The Runaway Scrape" was the prosaic name given this scramble to escape the wrath of the vengeful intruder from the south.

Only a few of the settlers were determined to stay.

The Parkers were among them.

Immediately after the fall of the Alamo, Sam Houston, the newly elected commander of the army of Texas, issued a call for volunteers to stem the tide of invasion.

Daniel Parker was one of those who responded.[3]

During the early days of April, Santa Anna continued his march to the northeast and burned the town of San Felipe on the banks of the Brazos. Houston's failure to challenge him there gave the Mexican commander even greater confidence.

On April 14 the major division of the Mexican army, led personally by Santa Anna, crossed the Brazos and continued its unimpeded movement. The president of Mexico then proceeded to establish his headquarters on a coastal plain bordering the San Jacinto River. There he set up camp.

Houston had kept close tabs on the movements of his opponent. Quickly, he moved his men toward Santa Anna's position. By April 20, the Texans were encamped on the same plain.

April 21 dawned clear and cool. By midafternoon, the feeling among the Mexicans that the Texans might attack had subsided. Houston sensed the time for action had come: he gave the command to advance, and the exasperated Texans swept through the camp of Santa Anna's unsuspecting soldiers. Most of the members of the division personally commanded by the president of Mexico were either captured or killed. Texan patrols began the task of rounding up those who had escaped the initial onslaught, and, by the next day, even El Presidente was a prisoner of war.[4]

Daniel Parker was at San Jacinto when Houston's army charged into the camp of the Mexican commander. He helped round up the stragglers following the conflict and was on hand the following day, when the victorious settlers discovered that along with other escapees they had captured the president of Mexico. Parker was among that vast majority of Texans who were confident that the detainment of Santa Anna was a guarantee of peace for the frontier.

A provisional government was established, and later in the year national elections were held in which a president, a vice-president, and a congress were chosen for the fledgling republic.

The settlers who had fled from Texas began to return. Those who had dared to stay took new courage, believing their land was secure from hostile attack.

But peace had not come to the Southwest. The major war for the control of Texas was about to begin.

The settlers who arrived in growing numbers from east of the Mississippi were still aliens in a land which long had been dominated by powerful native peoples. The Spaniards, who had arrived in the region three centuries earlier, had been able to make extensive accommodations to the lifestyle of the Indian. There had been conflict, but there had also been understanding; there had been armed clashes, but there had also been long periods of peace. While the Spaniard often overwhelmed the native inhabitants of the Southwest and sometimes sought to enslave them, there was interrelationship, often intermarriage, and generally broad areas of peaceful interaction.

When the Anglos began to arrive in strength, there was little willingness to accept or understand the heritage of the natives. This new wave of immigrants to the Southwest believed they could easily push back the Indian as their fathers and grandfathers had done along the eastern coast of the United States.

The Parkers had fought Indian tribes in Tennessee. Soon after their arrival in Texas, Silas and James Parker joined a militia company prepared to do battle with any native tribe which threatened Anglo settlement. The enemy, however, appeared to be primarily those who had come from south of the Rio Grande River: the ranger group was disbanded early in 1836.[5]

Knowing little about the military strength of the tribesmen of the South Plains, they naively assumed they could quickly rally a militia should the need arise. This was an assumption based on a complete ignorance of the strength and the tenacity of peoples such as the Comanches, the Apaches, and the Kiowas.

Those in the Parker migration, like most Anglo settlers, had no understanding and little knowledge of the people who had long inhabited the Texas prairies. The nomadic existence of these peoples was incomprehensible to immigrants coming into Texas from the United States.

Early travelers from east of the Sabine, who came in contact with Indians, reported them to be "the most degraded specimens of humanity" they had ever witnessed, basing their negative assessment on nothing other than the fact that they did not cultivate the land.[6] They were merely nomads to be displaced.

On the other hand, the natives of Texas saw the coming of the Anglo invasion not only as a deliberate encroachment upon their hunting grounds, but as a direct challenge to their very existence.

The building of settlements such as Parker's Fort was understood by the Indian as a challenge to his right to exist, a spear aimed toward the heartland of the area which had been willed to him by his forebears.

It was inevitable that the battle for the control of the Southwest would continue long after the last gun had been fired on the plain of San Jacinto.

Only days after the Texan victory over Santa Anna, the real war for control of the Southwest burst into full flame. This took the form of a raid by exasperated warriors on those they considered intruders into their territory. Like most incidents which spark the fire of war, this was not a planned action, but one of those events which represented years of smoldering resentment and misunderstanding.[7]

It was more than an incident. It was the signal fire for the intensification of bitter conflict between white settler and native inhabitant, a contest which would end in the complete defeat and near extermination of the weaker of the two.

This was the war which would be continued for forty years.

One member of the Parker family, Cynthia Ann, was destined to become the focal point of the early days of this contest. Little did anyone know that her son would be at the vortex of the final days of that long and bitter struggle.

IV.

Captive Journey

The trail led to the northwest.

The route of travel for both the captives from the raid on Fort Parker and their captors would have been a difficult trek under any circumstances.

For the marauding Indians it was an escape from the possible vengeance of their adversaries. They had inflicted damage on the enemy, whom they considered callous invaders of their territory. They were now in possession of the limited supplies which they could easily carry, and, of even greater importance, they had five hostages who might bring silver coins or goods of considerable value at some later date.

For the captives, it was a ride of terror.

Contemporary accounts indicate that both six-year-old John Parker and his nine-year-old sister, Cynthia Ann, had been placed on horseback behind raiding braves.[1] Once mounted, the riders left the area moving as rapidly as their ponies could travel.[2]

The two women captives were forced to leave the scene of the raid mounted in similar fashion behind other warriors. A fifth captive, the eighteen-month-old infant of one of the female hostages, was also spirited away. Since the time of the raid was placed by chroniclers at eight o'clock in the morning,[3] the captives began their trek before nine. Within an hour or two, the heat of late May became intense. This added to their agony.

The physical discomfort of the journey, however, was the least of the hostages' concerns. The sights and sounds of the reign of terror within the fort were fresh in their memories. The adult captives had witnessed the sufferings of their relatives and the tortured deaths of the men who had been scalped and mutilated. They knew that severe punishment awaited them should they be caught in an escape attempt. They had no choice other than to obey the commands of their captors.

By the time the full sunshine of noon had begun to take its toll on the hostages, they had become almost senseless from their experience. The fear of what might lie ahead for them added to their suffering. In desperation, the women and children clung to their captors on the fast moving horses as they continued their journey into the unknown.

Cynthia Ann and John Parker fared somewhat less severe treatment than the adult captives. Cynthia Ann did not witness the death of her father or the brutal killing of the men. Her mother, Lucy Parker, must have known what was happening from the moment the attack on the fort began. She was able to provide a place of safety for her brood in some recess within the fort. When the noise of the raid ceased, however, she sought to flee with her children from the fort hoping to escape through a back entrance of the enclosure.[4] Their effort to gain freedom was interrupted when she and her children were overtaken by several of the raiders a short distance from the fort.

Once mounted on Indian horses, Cynthia Ann, along with the other hostages, became human trophies of the raid. Her mother and the two remaining children would have become captives had it not been for the arrival of the Bates-Faulkenberry party. Fearing that the rescuers were followed by reinforcements, the raiders turned their horses to the north and rode away. Lucy Parker and her two younger children were spared.[5]

Rachel Plummer's narrative provides a detailed account of the events which followed the attack. According to her recollections, the Indians sought to evade potential pursuers by riding as rapidly as possible throughout the daylight hours of May 19. They did not stop to make camp until the middle of the night.

Plummer claimed she was beaten during the trek, and at night she was tied with "a platted thong round my arms and . . . a thong round my ankles."[6]

Both she and the other adult woman, Elizabeth Kellog, were abused during the journey. Her repeated mention of mistreatment might appear, at least in part, an effort to draw sympathy to herself. However, adult captives usually did receive harsh treatment during the initial stages of their captivity in order to enforce upon them the necessity of strict obedience to their captors.

Since Cynthia Ann had not reached puberty, she was not subject to the molestation experienced by the mature women. Both she and her brother would have been considered possible future members of a Comanche tribe rather than mere hostages subject to exchange. Captives, particularly younger ones, were sometimes selected for integration into the tribal structure.[7]

Cynthia Ann and her brother traveled the same route as the one described by Rachel Plummer, and although they were not abused because of their age, they suffered all of the difficulties of the trail.

During the night of May 19, all five captives were bound hand and foot with leather straps as they lay on the ground within the raiders' camp. At the first light of day on the following morning, the entire party continued the trip northward.

In addition to the discomforts of travel under such conditions, there was the agony of sunburn, which would become more intense each day of the protracted journey. This was always a problem for white women and children who were forced to undergo the difficulties of the trail. Comanches rode the trail with little or no clothing, and they expected their captives to do the same. Anglos who had been captured by Indians, particularly those who had known little previous exposure to the sun, experienced severe suffering under these conditions.[8]

Dolly Webster, a young white woman who was captured by Comanches in 1837, reported that "they stripped me of nearly all my clothes . . . they stripped my youngest child entirely naked."[9]

The removal of the clothing of captives was done, at least in part, under practical necessity. Plains Indians considered the extensive wearing apparel generally worn by Anglos, particularly women, as unnecessary encumbrance to rapid movement. Once stripped of their heavier garb, those who had been captured were believed to be capable of traveling rapidly with their captors so as to outdistance possible pursuers.

Ole Nystel, a captive of the Plains Indians during this period, declared that his clothing was "stripped off" leaving "my skin exposed to the sun causing my skin to blister."[10]

Removing clothes from hostages was done also as a means of subjugating and controlling captives who had been taken in raids. Indians were aware that weapons could be concealed in the folds of the garments of Anglo hostages. The nudity of captured prisoners was a practical means of protecting the captors.

Since Cynthia Ann and John, along with the other captives, were required to ride naked during their journey, their discomfort increased in intensity with each new day of travel as the late May sun fell upon their blistering skin.

The Dollbeare account indicated concern upon the part of the captors of Dolly Webster that they might be followed: each day for four days "we pursued on our journey until midnight [and] when we stopped, the Indians lay down without fire or refreshment."[11]

The Parker captors demanded a similar type of forced travel. Comanches made a practice of traveling as far as possible until they believed themselves out of danger. Only then did they slack their pace.[12] The hostages continued to be herded to the north with no food and minimal water. Hunger pangs would have added to their discomfort since there was no time to secure fresh food.

On the fourth day, the travelers who had been carrying their captives toward the north "turned more east," where, according to

Plummer, they "reached a grand prairie."[13]

The captive journey continued across the Red River into an area where the Indians felt secure from possible retaliation. An encampment was established for the purpose of distributing the human trophies among the several tribal groups involved in the raid. This event must have taken place north of the Red River, possibly in the Wichita Mountain area of Oklahoma.

Plummer claimed that a half dozen other tribes, in addition to the Comanches, were participants in the raid. She listed the following Indian groups among her captors: "Cadoes, Tywaconies, Keacheys, Wakos, Towash, some Beadies."[14]

Although Plummer's record was accurate on most details, there are flaws in her published journals. She stated that six to seven hundred Indians took part in the raid and that the attack was the result of a decision made at a major consultation of Indian peoples.[15] Such a large group could not have traveled together, living off the land for such a prolonged period. The Parker manuscript placed the attack party at no more than 100, a more accurate figure.[16] It is also unlikely that as many tribes were represented in the gathering as she claimed or that the attack on Fort Parker was conducted as the result of a decision made by a confederated council of Indian people.

There were several Comanche sub-tribes present, however, at the encampment where the hostages and the booty were distributed. On the fourth day of the trek, the infant, James, was separated from his mother, Rachel.[17] The mother, the son, and the Parker brother and sister each became the property of one of the several Comanche groups involved in the raid.

One of these was the warlike band known as the Quohadi.[18] Cynthia Ann became their property. Elizabeth Kellog was handed over to another Indian group and eventually became a hostage of members of the Kitchawa tribe.

There is no further written evidence of the immediate fate of Cynthia Ann after she was separated from the other captives. The nine-year-old daughter of the Parkers, however, would have undergone experiences similar to those recorded by other captives who later returned to civilization to write about their adventures among the South Plains Indians.

One of the most vivid of these is the account written by Rachel Plummer. Following her separation from the other captives, her owners carried her to the northwest.[19] She described in detail her continued journey into Indian territory, giving an indication of the route. She traveled through an area where there was no timber continuing in a northwesterly direction. This would have meant a trek through western Oklahoma, moving along the waters of the Canadian River and then northwest across the High Plains. Her journey then took her through the Oklahoma panhandle into what is now Colorado, where she reported seeing snow-capped mountains.[20]

She was assigned as a slave to a tall Indian, who, because of his height, was known as Tall-as-the-Sky. By July, she had been forced to travel "in the snow mountains where it is perpetual snow."[21]

Throughout her account, she claimed that she continued to receive mistreatment insisting that "they whipped me a number of times."[22]

Dolly Webster's recollections spoke of severe treatment which was meted out to her by Indians who "claimed the privilege of inflicting blows on me."[23] However, her record admits that other captives, particularly younger captives, received much better treatment. Possibly adult women prisoners such as Plummer and Webster were intent on making it very clear in their published statements that they had only remained among the Indians under duress of the most severe sort.

In October, Rachel Plummer gave birth to another child. In her account she described the unassisted natal ordeal: she was able to cut the umbilical cord with a sharp stick she found among the grapevines where she had hidden, fearing the infant would not be accepted by her masters. She claimed that her fears were well founded: soon after the birth, the child was taken from her breasts and strangled by her captors. When breathing continued, the body was pulled through rugged vegetation until all signs of life were gone.[24]

Winter came and Rachel Plummer found herself in the high
north country. At one point she saw a large gathering of Indians
and was told that it was a war council preparing to make slaves of
many whites.[25]

During her captivity, however, the only results of martial operations she observed were five bodies of Osage Indians, brought
into the camp dangling from ponies to prove the prowess of her Comanche captors.[26]

At last contact was made with a group of Mexican traders who
were willing to pay for the release of Rachel. Silver coins were exchanged, and she was taken on a seventeen-day journey to Santa
Fe. There she was welcomed into the home of a Col. William Don-
oho, who paid the trader for his act of redemption. Passage was secured for her back to her home in Texas by way of Independence,
Missouri.[27]

After reporting that she arrived at her father's home on February 19, 1838, she declared: "My constitution is broke." She concluded her journal with these pathetic words: "Where is my poor
little James Pratt!"[28]

James did survive the sojourn among the Comanches with far
less difficulty than his mother. He was returned to Anglo civilization, along with John Parker, through the efforts of the United
States military, which, according to the Parker manuscript,
brought the two boys to Fort Gibson. It was there that their grandfather was able to contact them and bring them both back to the
family settlement in Texas.[29]

The fourth of the hostages, Elizabeth Kellog, was sold by the
Kitchawas to a group of Indians who appeared with her in Nacog-
doches, where the residents purchased her for the sum of $150.[30]

By this time the captives of the raid on Fort Parker were all accounted for with the exception of one. Nothing was known about
the daughter of Lucy and the slain Silas Parker.

Based on Rachel Plummer's report, the Anglo contemporaries
of Cynthia Ann could only imagine what she might be suffering if
she had survived the initial hardships of a captive journey.

V.

Sinthy Ann Remains

Late May of 1836 soon gave way to the hot, dry days of June.

On the High Plains the heat of the summer sun bore down mercilessly upon Cynthia Ann as she and the other captives from Fort Parker were forced to travel further into Indian territory. By this time she had been parceled out to one of the several tribal groups of the South Plains, the Quohadi Comanches.

Back on the Texas frontier, once the initial shock of the raid had begun to subside, there was only limited hope for the survival of any of the hostages. Cynthia Ann's family knew only that she had been carried away by her Indian captors, and that, if she still lived, she was somewhere in the vast expanses of the sun-drenched land beyond the frontier.

When the news of the raid had been passed from settlement to settlement, most Texans realized that there was little which could be done to avenge those who had been killed. They also knew that any effort to bring back the hostages by military force would be futile.

Texas had just begun its decade of independence as a republic. In its struggle for existence the young nation faced far greater problems than that of the fate of white captives in Indian territory.

A provisional government had been established in an effort to bring order out of the uncertainties of the year 1836. Headed by David Burnet, the fledgling republic began to make strides toward demonstrating its ability to survive. Sam Houston had left Texas to be treated for wounds he had received during the fighting at San Jacinto. This left the nation with a temporary void of leadership.

Burnet responded to the challenge with determination. He was faced, however, with a variety of problems. There was the threat of another major invasion from Mexico. By the end of June, rumors of Mexican forces returning to Texas soil were arriving almost daily.[1]

There were serious internal problems. The army of frontiersmen which had overcome Santa Anna at San Jacinto had evaporated. These citizen soldiers found it necessary to return home to tend the crops which had been planted earlier in the spring. In place of the patriot band commanded by Houston, there was an aggregation of adventurers from the United States who had become nothing more than an unruly mob.[2]

In July, Provisional President Burnet called for an election which would establish a permanent government for the republic.[3] But the process of building a new political structure for the recently declared nation was a slow one. It would be the end of the year before a congress and properly elected executives could assume power.

In the face of threats from without and turmoil within, there was little time for concern over the condition of hostages being held by nomadic tribes hundreds of miles from the centers of settlement.

The Parker family, however, did not forget those who had been spirited away from them.

In a statement written eight years after the raid, James W. Parker described the efforts which his family had made to reclaim their lost daughter. He made it clear that although the government of Texas could do little to aid them, the Parkers continued to do everything possible to bring her back home.

In 1844 he summed up the situation with these words:

Only Sinthy Ann remains in captivity. Parker published and offered a reward of $200 each for the prisoners in order to try to enlist the energy of the traders to reach his friends. He also afterwards offered an additional reward of $300 each for any prisoner that might be brought in by the traders. This was the moving cause that brought in his daughter Mrs. Plummer.[4]

He sent this document to Mirabeau Lamar, who by that time had become an ex-president of the Republic of Texas.

The Parker offer of $200 for the return of any one of the captives was a substantial sum under the circumstances. Since hostages were often taken and held for a time by Indian tribes for ransom, a unique type of commerce had developed. Traders, who knew the sites where the South Plains nomads camped, would make contact with a tribe known to be holding white captives, offer silver or goods of value to the Indians in exchange, and then return the hostage to Anglo civilization. Of course, adequate compensation for the trader from relatives was necessary for the completion of this transaction. This was the process which brought Rachel Plummer to Santa Fe. In recounting her adventures, Rachel appeared proud that silver coins rather than goods of lesser value had purchased her release.[5]

Elizabeth Kellog's return to white settlement for a ransom of $150 was less than the Parker offer. This method of redemption, even with the more generous sum offered, had no impact, however, on the captivity of Cynthia Ann.

When the $200 offer did not bring her back, the additional bounty of $300 boosted the amount offered for her return to a sum which was an attractive prize for any frontier trader.

The $500 offer represented a sizable sum for the Parkers. The currency of the Republic of Texas had little value at the time. The redemption money offered by James Parker would have been payable only in United States silver, since Indian traders would have had no use for the Texas red-back, the legal tender of the youthful nation.[6]

The Parkers, along with most other Texans at this time, had land and property but very little negotiable currency. Their offer was a genuinely sacrificial effort to effect Cynthia's return.

Mirabeau B. Lamar, who had served as the second president of the republic, was sympathetic with the Parker family's wish to reclaim their kin, but there was nothing he could do but file the carefully written manuscript among his extensive papers. This information, however, gave him some assurance that his policy of vigorous prosecution of Indian depredations during his three-year term as president of Texas had been a correct one.

When he had taken over the executive office from his predecessor, Sam Houston, late in 1838, he had vowed to do everything possible to protect Texas settlers from raids such as the one on the Parker settlement. In a statement to the Congress of the Republic immediately after taking office, Lamar declared that protection from marauding Indians was a duty of his administration. "The poorest citizen," he stated, "holds as sacred a claim upon the government for safety and security as does the man who lives in ease."[7]

The Texas Congress responded by authorizing the president to accept eight companies of mounted volunteers for six months and appropriated $75,000 for a militia. Another $5,000 was set aside for establishing a fifty-six-member ranger corps.[8] The militia was only a temporary measure. The creation of the Texas Rangers, who were soon to become legendary for their exploits in taming the frontier, was, however, a permanent action: they were destined to play a primary role in the Forty Year War between Indians and whites.

Lamar's policies toward the Native Americans represented a dramatic change from those of his predecessor. Sam Houston, the first elected president of Texas, had lived among Indians and he understood them in a way in which few Anglos could. He had personally negotiated a treaty with a band of Cherokees living in East Texas in February 1836, giving his solemn word that they would get a clear title to the land they claimed.[9]

However, when the Republic of Texas was finally established and a congress had been duly elected, there was little interest among white Texans in ratifying the agreement between Houston and the chief of the Cherokees.

By the time the first congress met, there was widespread

knowledge of the massacre at Fort Parker, which had taken place as Texas first became conscious of its nationhood. This event was a determining factor in the new leaders' decision to deal harshly with all Indians. The relatively peaceful Cherokees of East Texas would suffer because of the actions of a few of their distant cousins. White settlers were in no mood to make a distinction between the different Indian bands once the horror stories of the Fort Parker raid were generally known.

In 1838, Rachel Plummer's dramatic account of her capture by Comanches appeared in print and was widely read both in Texas and the United States.[10] Her vivid description of the attack on Fort Parker, and her account of the brutal killing of her infant, added to the Anglo desire to retaliate. The tribesmen of the plains, whom she claimed had beaten and raped her, became the ultimate villains. Her descriptions of her own sufferings simply added fuel to the flames of hatred for the Comanche.

The war against the Indian continued to increase in intensity. Lamar, acting upon the authorization given him by Congress, called for volunteers for a militia to deal with the Cherokees of East Texas.[11] Maj. B. G. Walters was instructed to lead an army into the land claimed by the Native Americans and build a fort at Grand Saline. Chief Bowles responded by mobilizing his warriors and then proceeded to order Walters out of the area. For the Texans this was another act of hostility in the escalating conflict.[12]

A commission of the Texas government, sent to negotiate with the Cherokees, offered them payment for their land and improvements on the condition they leave Texas. Initially, the Cherokee leadership agreed to the proposal. When it became apparent that the Indians had no immediate plans for departure, the Texans assembled a force of five hundred volunteers, led by Gen. Kelsey Douglass, to enforce the demands of the government of the republic.

On July 15, 1839, as the two armed groups eyed each other, fighting erupted. Chief Bowles was shot down in the initial action, and in the two weeks which followed, Cherokee resistance was crushed in a brutal effort to destroy or capture the entire tribe. The survivors were then unceremoniously marched out of Texas.[13]

The expulsion of the Cherokees merely served to set off a fresh round of Indian-settler conflicts. The president of the republic soon received reports of raids on Anglo settlements as far south as the Victoria area near the coast. One South Texas resident reported to Lamar that Comanches had "killed many of the citizens and all the horses . . . the town of Linnville had been burnt to the ground." [14]

In 1840 a tragic event known as "The Council House Fight" occurred in San Antonio. In January, three Comanche chiefs entered the town and approached the militia commander, Henry Karnes, with a request for a treaty. Karnes replied that there could be no peace until he was certain all white captives had been released. In response to his demand, the visiting chiefs returned soon afterward with a fifteen-year-old girl, Matilda Lockhart, who had been a Comanche prisoner. She showed obvious marks of mistreatment. [15]

This effort at peaceful negotiation, however, was not satisfactory to the Texans. Well aware that other Anglos, including Cynthia Ann, were in the hands of various Indian tribes, they demanded that all captives be brought to San Antonio. A Comanche spokesman replied that there were many other tribes who may be holding additional captives over which they had no control.

In the midst of the increasingly tense situation, one Indian retorted: "How do you like that answer?"

With this, the exasperation of the Texans gave way to violence. A command was given to cordon off the area and take prisoners. Bedlam broke loose; even the Comanche women joined in the desperate fight. The end result of this uneven battle was the death, wounding, or imprisonment of the entire Indian contingent while fifteen whites were either killed or seriously wounded.

Vinton Lee James, who later recorded his recollections of this event, declared that "The Courthouse Fight . . . was precipitated . . . by a refusal on the part of the Comanches to bring in their captives," which in the year 1840 would have included Cynthia Ann. [16]

Open and unrelenting warfare now developed. No longer were there any efforts at peaceful negotiation. Any of the Indians who knew of the conflict in San Antonio believed the Native American effort to seek some form of peace had been answered with violence. Anglos, on the other hand, felt they were justified in hunting down and destroying Comanches whenever possible because of the mistreatment of white captives like Matilda Lockhart, and the continued enslavement, it was believed at the time, of Cynthia Ann. This further added to the hatred and distrust which had been generated by accounts of the massacre at Fort Parker and the passionate writings of Rachel Plummer.

In spite of the increasing crescendo of conflict, the Parkers continued their efforts to reclaim Cynthia Ann. One report indicated contact was made with the tribe with whom Cynthia Ann was living at about the time James Parker's statement was penned. This was an obvious response to the prize money which had been offered for her return to white civilization. A group of traders, accompanied by an Indian guide, "fell in with a band of Comanches" and saw Cynthia Ann. This initial contact with the daughter of the Parkers took place in the early 1840s after the bounty for her release had become known on the frontier.[17]

One of the members of the trading party later reported that he offered goods worth several hundred dollars for her. However, the Indians would not consider the offer since "she was claimed by a chief, who refused to give her up." The account concluded with the statement that Cynthia Ann "would run away and hide from those who tried to ransom her."[18]

James Parker wrote his plea for help in the final days of the republic. He concluded his plaintive statement with a declaration that he had sought Cynthia Ann's return "with energy 'til his health became so poor he could go no further."[19]

One account indicates that at the urging of his family, John Parker, Cynthia's younger brother, also taken captive in the Fort Parker raid, made an effort to find her. He later claimed he made contact with her, but she refused to accompany him back to white civilization.[20]

Daniel Parker, who had led the company of pilgrims to Texas, died in December 1844, immediately after James had penned the statement he sent to Mirabeau Lamar.[21] With the death of Daniel and the loss of health by James Parker, all effective efforts by the family to bring about the return of the lost Parker girl came to an end.

Efforts to negotiate her release continued by the United States government, but even these were abandoned soon after 1847. Robert S. Neighbors, a special Indian agent, reported that he had reason to believe Cynthia Ann was being held by a Comanche band which generally ranged along the headwaters of the Red River and with whom agents had little or no intercourse. Neighbors had talked with friendly chiefs about the possibility of returning her to white civilization. However, they had assured him that it would require considerable force to bring her back to her natal family.[22]

From all indications, the white daughter of the Parkers was destined to remain a Comanche for the rest of her natural life.

VI.

A Trophy Of Conquest

The sun comes early to the land in June.

On the prairie, where there is little escape from the direct rays of the sun, the heat becomes intense before noon and continues unabated through most of the daylight hours. In the year 1836, even the vast grasslands which had been made verdant by rains earlier in the season were, by this time, taking on a somber, yellowish hue in response to the increasing warmth and inevitable aridness of late spring.

This was the season that Cynthia Ann made her forced journey to the High Plains.

The route of travel led westward from the raiders' rendezvous point near the Red River, a hundred or more miles north of the outer fringes of white settlement. Because of the abundant rain throughout the area earlier in the year, buffalo herds had returned for grazing to the lower portion of the South Plains. The great animals would have taken advantage of the natural grass upon the level prairies surrounding the upper waters of rivers which flowed toward the distant Gulf of Mexico.

When the buffalo herds moved southward, the Indians of the plains followed. Unable to exist in the semidesert conditions of the area, except where the massive animals were in abundance, the various Comanche tribes were uniquely dependent upon the prairie beasts for all of the basic necessities of life.

Cynthia Ann began her journey toward the High Plains before the end of May. Her captors would trek toward the west, anticipating joining their fellow Comanches at some point where the buffalo had led them.

This portion of the ride in captivity took place at a less frantic pace than that of the first five days of the journey. There was no longer the fear of being overtaken by a Texan militia. The Indians were secure in the territory they considered their own, for this was a land into which few whites dared come.

The trail led westward along the waters of the Red River. There was time to secure food en route and to establish camp sites near the stream, which brought consistent refreshment to the vast, unsettled area. By following the river, not only was there adequate water for the band of natives who owned the young, female white, but there was game for hunting.

Each morning camp was broken at an early hour. Movement began upon the unmarked trail along a route which paralleled the stream. With the sun behind the trekkers, the early hours of travel were easy ones. In midafternoon the determination would be made to establish camp in a place where game could be found. For the first time, the young Parker captive would witness the efficiency of the bow and arrow as a means of providing food. When there was ample time after the hunt, a fire was built from river driftwood. The travelers who had eaten but little in the early days of the journey north and west from Fort Parker were able to dine at leisure before nightfall. It was then that sleep came quickly after the exhaustion of the trail.

No longer was it necessary to tie the captive by hand and foot. In the vast land in which she found herself, Cynthia Ann knew instinctively that her only hope for survival was that of following her captors into whatever existence lay ahead for her. There was no inning and certainly no possibility of successful escape.

Hostages often come, in time, to accept and admire those who ave taken them captive. Cynthia Ann, in the midst of fearing for er life, began the inevitable process of accepting the culture which ad forcibly removed her from her natal family.

By mid-June the party reached the eastern boundary of the igh Plains. At the junction of the Pease River with the main ream of the Red, the travelers veered to the southwest in order to ake contact with fellow Comanches who were, by that time, on e southern reaches of the plains. There, amid the copper red uffs, which provide the source of the sediment responsible for the ame of the river, began the final stage of the young Parker's jour-ey into the domain of the Indian.

Following the depressions carved from the land itself, the trail d the captors of Cynthia Ann to high flatlands through the rug-ed break country in the direction of Palo Duro. At last the gradual ssent was made to the levelness of the prairie. Travel became eas-r since there were no irregularities or steep up slopes. For the outhful captive there was the feeling of being hopelessly dwarfed y the sheer majesty of the land before her. The endless sea of buf-lo grass stretched to the horizon and far beyond. Overhead was e massiveness of the high vaulted, blue sky which arched above ith only an occasional distant cloud to question its continuity.[1]

The band of trekkers moved far enough to the west to join the ain body of one of the most nomadic of all of the South Plains In-ians, the Quohadi. It was there, among this roving, warlike peo-le, that Cynthia Ann was destined to grow to maturity and spend ost of her adult life.[2]

Cynthia Ann's experiences during this initial period of captiv-y were similar to those reported by other female captives. How-ver, because of her age, she was treated with greater deference an hostages who had been taken chiefly for the purpose of secur-g ransom for their freedom. Since there is evidence that the Co-anches considered young, female whites to be potentially highly rolific, and thus valuable in assuring the continuation of the ibe,[3] Cynthia would have received the treatment due a valued trophy of conquest. Other captives, such as T. A. Babb, who were considered candidates for full membership in the tribe, were treated much more gently than hostages destined for exchange.[4]

The process of adaptation into a nomadic life on the prairie was a traumatic experience for the young girl. She underwent the same natural hardships reported by Rachel Plummer, whose experiences shed light on the early years on the plains for the young Parker captive. Although Cynthia Ann may have been treated with some degree of deference, she experienced all of the difficulties of integration into tribal life. She knew fear and fatigue, hunger and privation. She suffered from exposure to the elements, exhaustion after endless hours of travel, and the gnawing anxiety of wondering what might lie ahead.

Recovering from her initial exposure to the sun was one of the less complex problems for her during the early weeks as a Comanche captive. Later accounts indicate that she was recognized as a white woman by Ross' rangers largely because her blue eyes gave away her identity — an identity which, by that time, had become obscured because her skin coloring was similar to that of other members of the Quohadi tribe.[5]

Although Cynthia Ann suffered in the process of developing a skin tint adaptable to her existence on the prairie, much of her pain would have been eased by the application of some type of salve or grease from the buffalo.

Rachel Plummer reported that extensive healing methods for skin discomforts had been developed by her Comanche captors.[6] Sanapia, the daughter of a traditional Comanche medicine woman, described the use of "salves and ointments" which were "applied with four movements of the hand."[7] Ease of this sort was brought to Cynthia Ann by similar methods of relief. This would have been an early factor in conditioning the young Anglo to an acceptance of the life in which she found herself.

After the completion of her journey into Indian territory, Cynthia Ann was handed over to a mature woman of the tribe for both discipline and instruction. Accounts of the experiences of other Comanche captives indicated that each white hostage was assigned a guardian immediately after entering into the life of the tribe. This person was usually a woman without children.[8]

Cynthia Ann was placed under the care of such a person who then became her mentor, and who was responsible to the tribal leadership for her future development. She was fed, instructed, and disciplined by the older Indian woman to whom she had been assigned.

Although captives were often traded between Indian tribal groups and then sold to a professional hostage purchaser for money or goods, there is no indication that Cynthia Ann was ever treated as a captive subject to ransom. Because of her age and her reproductive potential, she was accepted into the tribal structure of the Quohadi.

Immediately after the beginning of her residence among the Plains Indians, she began the process of learning the skills necessary for life upon the prairie. Initially, she was assigned tasks which required little skill but were essential to tribal existence: wood gathering, fire building, assisting in the preparation of food and cooking, and the maintenance and care of utensils and equipment.

This integration process has been described by other white captives in the literature which has survived from the mid-nineteenth century. There were several Anglos who spent anywhere from a few months to several years as captives of the Comanches: Ole Nystel,[9] T. A. Babb,[10] Nelson Lee,[11] and others who related similar experiences as captives during this period.[12] These accounts provide information about the circumstances of Cynthia Ann's early years on the South Plains. In addition, the records of several female hostages add to this information: Rachel Plummer, Dolly Webster, Jane Adeline Wilson,[13] and the account of the captivity of two adult females, a Mrs. Horn and a Mrs. Harris.[14]

Gradually, Cynthia Ann was introduced to more advanced skills necessary for life on the prairie. Her tribal mentor was responsible for this initial learning process, in the same way that Mrs. Harris was placed under the care of a woman who served as her task master and instructor.[15]

Cynthia Ann learned from her mistress the arts of curing hides and making necessary clothing items. Jane Adeline Wilson's account reported that she was required to make robes, bags, and other products from buffalo hide.[16] Similar tasks were assigned to the young Parker.

Early in her life upon the prairie, Cynthia was provided with buffalo skin apparel.[17] The clothing she wore at the time of capture was discarded early in the trek to the northwest. Since she was a child at the time she joined the main body of the Quohadi, her first clothing would have been of the simplest kind, consisting of nothing more than a portion of a buffalo hide. Such would have provided protection from the late evening chill of the High Plains and also would have served as cover for sleeping. As she matured, and before the time she was accepted as an adult, more adequate apparel would be available to her, consisting of animal skin which had been prepared both for comfort and for fit.

As she approached puberty, she was expected to wear clothing of her own making which covered the lower portion of her body. In addition, she would possess a robe for protection from the elements.

Besides making her own clothing, as well as assisting in providing robes and garments for other members of the tribe, Cynthia was required to master a wide variety of crafts which were necessary for existence on the plains. She would have been adept at producing implements necessary for the trail, which might have been used by raiding warriors seeking to push back the tide of white settlement. The actual weapons of war, however, were always crafted by individual braves who would trust no female in the preparation of instruments for battle. The young Parker girl also received instruction in the manufacture of items for domestic use, almost all of which were the products of the buffalo.[18]

Her introduction into the worklife of a Comanche nomad took place quickly. It is likely that she learned rapidly, and that she made a determined effort to be accepted as a member of the Quohadi band. She possessed a high degree of intelligence; her Parker ancestors were noted for "splendid intellect."[19] This was a factor which would have assisted her in mastering techniques essential for adaptation to life as an Indian. Unlike many other female captives, she was readily integrated into Comanche tribal life.

Early in her experiences upon the prairie, she would have accepted an appellation by which she was known to other members of the tribe. Several possible Indian names for her appear in records based on Comanche tradition: "Naduah," "Preloch," "Norah." These appellations, if they were used at all, were possibly little more than nicknames or informal titles by which she may have been known at different times during her years on the prairie.[20]

The uncertainty about the name she used as an Indian raises an interesting probability: she must have insisted upon being called by her family name, and it is likely that she continued her natal surname throughout her life as an Indian. One of the earliest reports of contacts with her captors by Indian commissioners referred to her as "a girl . . . known as [one of] the Parker children."[21] The fact that her son, Quanah, knew and accepted the name of Parker would indicate that she must have retained at least this portion of her white heritage. A. E. Butterfield stated that Quanah chose the name of his mother, Parker.[22] R. B. Marcy referred to her in 1854 as "a white woman among the Middle Comanches by the name of Parker."[23]

Within three to four years after her capture, Cynthia Ann reached puberty and was deemed ready for marriage. Captives such as Rachel Plummer and Elizabeth Kellog were retained simply as slaves and hostages. But efforts were made to integrate others into the tribal structure. Dolly Webster reported that after she had lived for a time as an Indian captive, she was "ushered into a large ring, encircled by Indians and had to undergo the ceremony of being made a Comanche."[24] Those who were willing to learn the skills necessary for survival on the prairie became candidates for full incorporation into the tribe. Ole Nystel believed he was considered to be a candidate for acceptance into Comanche culture. He reported that he was given opportunities to learn the crafts which were essential for life on the plains. When he proved himself capable of participation in events such as the buffalo hunt, a mate was sought for him. If he had accepted this offer, he would have then become a part of the tribe.[25]

A husband was sought for the maturing Parker girl at an early age, since the production of children was essential to the survival of the Quohadi people. Her nuptial readiness occurred at about the year 1840.

Peta Nocona was a young brave at the time who was on the way to becoming a leader in battle and eventually a war chief. As the young Parker girl matured, she was regarded as a fitting wife for a promising warrior because of the mystique which Comanche culture had developed concerning the prolificacy of white women. Nocona selected Cynthia Ann from the marriageable females available. He then made arrangements with her guardian to take her to his lodge.

One contemporary account of Comanche life stated that when a brave decided on a wife, he would discuss his decision with the father or guardian of the woman he had chosen. Once assent had been given to the proposal by the adult responsible for the young woman, "she would then be handed over without dissent."[26] Another account which reflects Comanche oral tradition stated simply that Cynthia Ann was "married . . . by Indian custom to Peta Nokoni . . ."[27]

Before a male could take a wife, he was required to prove himself worthy of propagating offsprings. Nystel recorded that after passing puberty, a potential bridegroom would be required to undergo some type of ordeal, such as "lying motionless for hours" while members of the tribe "danced around him."[28] This rite, however, was only imposed upon future warriors in lieu of having proved themselves in battle, something which Nocona would have done early in his career.

By the act of taking the young, female white into his lodge, he declared her to be his mate. It was this simple mating process which established Cynthia Ann as a wife of Peta Nocona.

The decision of a prospective husband to take a mate, while not accompanied with a formal ceremony of marriage, did include a public declaration of nuptial intent.[29] This was accomplished by the act of leading the bridal prospect from the tepee in which she had been residing to his own dwelling. Such an act was generally performed in a manner to make a majority of the tribe aware that a particular brave had taken a young female of the tribe as a wife.

Cynthia Ann took this ritualistic walk, trailing properly behind Peta Nocona. Upon entering his tepee, she acknowledged her allegiance to the male who had chosen her by submitting herself to him in the anticipation of the production of an offspring. She had been carefully instructed by her female mentor in the necessity of pleasing her warrior mate and of accepting her position as a producer of Comanche children. This she did readily, eagerly seeking to be a satisfying sexual partner to her husband. The act of consummation completed the contract between the two: it was a binding agreement which was intended to last for the remainder of her life.

Capt. R. B. Marcy's account, written while Cynthia Ann was still living with the Quohadi, stated that her husband and children were "all that she held most dear."[30] Apparently, she accepted the full seriousness of her marriage contract and sought to be both a pleasing and a responsible wife to the brave who had claimed her.

The nuptial act itself was her final and complete acceptance of her position as a part of the tribe. This was her pledge of willingness not only to bear children by her warrior husband for the continuation of the tribe, but to become in every respect a Quohadi Indian.[31] In the words of a knowledgeable contemporary, "she adopted all the habits and peculiarities of the Comanches."[32]

Since the Plains Indians were polygamous, she eventually shared the tepee of Nocona with one or more other wives. However, because of her age and the likely age of her husband, she was probably the first wife of the warrior Nocona. Since he was in his prime of leadership in 1860, and probably lived for several years after that time, given the average life span of a warring Comanche, he must have been a young brave, probably not having reached the age of twenty, at the time Cynthia Ann became marriageable. This would indicate that she was not only his first wife, but that she held her position as primary wife to him throughout her years as a Quohadi.

Her first child, born no later than the middle of the 1840s, was given the name Quanah, meaning "Sweet Aroma."[33]

An Indian tradition which has been preserved in a manuscript in the Quanah Papers in the Archives of Fort Sill declared that the birth site of Cynthia Ann's first son was Cedar Lake, located twenty miles south of the present town of Brownfield, Texas.[34] This information not only indicates the importance that later Comanches attached to the birth of Quanah, but also gives some insight into the locale of Quohadi wanderings during this period.

Another male birth occurred soon afterward, when a second son was born to Cynthia Ann. This child was given the name Pecos,[35] probably named for the river which watered a portion of the territory within the Comanche range. The birth of two sons establi hed her as a worthy primary wife of a virile warrior.

Soon after Cynthia Ann proved her allegiance to the life she had adopted by bearing Comanche children, a ceremony of acceptance into the tribe was performed in her behalf. An act indicating full integration of an individual into a South Plains tribe often took place after the candidate had proven a willingness to be a part of the Indian way of life. Dollbeare's account of Dolly Webster's ritual of acceptance into a Comanche band during this same period was indicative of what happened to the wife of Nocona.[36]

One such rite which was practiced in the South Plains Indian culture involved the burning of tightly bound clumps of cedar bark. By this act, the person was declared to be a part of a particular tribe or a family grouping. The smoke from the smoldering cedar was allowed to penetrate the area where the individual was present, indicating blessing and complete acceptance. It is likely that the ritual of the Cedar Smoke took place for Cynthia Ann to clearly show that the Parker captive was no longer an alien subject to possible exchange: she was from that time forward a Quohadi Comanche.[37]

By the mid-1840s, Cynthia Ann was established as the wife of a leading Comanche brave and the mother of future Quohadi raiders. She not only was expected to bear and raise children but was still required to learn and practice the crafts of the Plains Indians considered essential for existence.

Evidence from mid-nineteenth-century accounts of these nomads of the Llano Estacado completes the depiction of the life Cynthia Ann lived during this period.

She was, by this time, an excellent horsewoman, even though

she was not expected to ride bareback in the fashion of a warrior of the tribe. She was a groomer of horses, giving special care to the horse of Peta Nocona.[38] And she continued to master the crafts related to making use of buffalo, not only for food but for all of the other necessities of life.

In this buffalo-dependent society, when the animal existed in great numbers, it was the woman's responsibility to utilize the results of the hunt. Although bison hunting was a year-round occupation, this activity reached a peak in the fall of each year, when the animals were in their prime. Then it was that the great hunts took place which provided food, clothing, and garments for protection from the elements for the difficult winter months which were to come.[39]

Once the kill had taken place, the women of the tribe were expected to scrape and prepare the buffalo leather from which they made robes, bags, and other products. All of the objects for everyday use, such as implements, thongs, and various sorts of bands and straps, were manufactured from the results of the hunt. The Comanche woman was expected to skin the animals, prepare the hides, and then produce these all-important items.

Even housing for these Indians depended upon securing large quantities of the pelts of the plains animals. Some ten to fifteen skins were necessary to make a single tepee.[40] These were placed on long poles to build structures which could easily be erected or quickly taken apart for removal to a new campsite. Both the erection and the maintenance of these basic living facilities were among the tasks assigned to the women of the tribe.

Responsibilities such as these were a part of the lifestyle which Cynthia Ann accepted as she became fully integrated into the tribe. By the middle years of the 1840s, the Parker girl who had been snatched from her natal family amid violence and bloodshed was a mature member of the Quohadi Comanches.

She was even more: she was the bearer of Indian children and a wife of one of the fiercest of the warriors of the South Plains, Peta Nocona.

VII.

The Unspoken Negative

Anson Jones, the final president of the Republic of Texas, stood solemnly in front of the simple building which had been designated as a national capitol. Several hundred persons had gathered in the frontier village of Austin to witness the end of a nation.

"The final act in this great drama is now performed," Jones declared. "The Republic of Texas is no more."[1]

It was February 16, 1846.

A decade earlier, Texas had declared itself an independent nation, but on this day the republic would cease to exist.

Amid the booming of cannon, the flag with its single star was lowered ceremoniously and the Stars and Stripes of the United States were unfurled.[2]

Even in the somberness of the occasion, there were great expectations for those who had gathered to witness this event. The United States had finally consented to accept Texas as a state of the Union, and the people of the republic had declared their willingness to become a part of the larger nation. No longer was Texas merely a buffer zone between the American states and enemies to the south and the west.

Since no major effort had been mounted by Mexico in recent years against the republic, there were few, by this time, who feared a serious attempt at invasion from the south. However, the realities of frontier life made it apparent that a far more troublesome enemy existed to the west: the powerful Indians of the South Plains.

Most settlers on the frontier considered the fierce Comanche tribes, who dominated the western portion of Texas, as the real enemy. Possibly this was more of a reason for the vigorously independent Texans to agree to a union with the United States than any frontiersman of the time would have acknowledged.

The warfare between Indian and Anglo along the fringes of white settlement had not ceased. There had been trouble between the two cultures from the very beginning, but these early Texans were too absorbed with the conflict with Mexico to recognize the fact they had invaded Indian territory and the real war was yet to be. It was not until the facts concerning the raid on Fort Parker were generally known that the seriousness of this contest between Texas and the Comanche nation became apparent to most Texans.

The war continued throughout the decade of the life of the republic. It would not cease, however, with the lowering of the Lone Star flag.

The Forty Year War had only completed its first decade.

The limited resources of the youthful nation had never been sufficient to guarantee any measure of security for the settlers on the Texas frontier. Now the boundaries of the United States included the territory which had long been controlled by the tribesmen of the South Plains. Those who feared the onslaughts of the Comanches took encouragement from the fact that Texas had become a part of a nation which had both the resources and the willingness to conquer the Indian. The war with the natives of the plains could be won.

It would only be after the United States had conquered Mexico, however, that the full force of American military strength would be turned toward the nomads of the prairie who continued to

be a barrier to white settlement. The major battles of the prolonged
contest between the two cultures were yet to be fought.

During the years that Texans had experimented with independence, Cynthia Ann had matured as a member of the Quohadi. By
the time Gen. Zachary Taylor had moved his American army into
northern Mexico and had overpowered the Mexican defenses outside of Monterrey,[3] the girl who had been captured in the raid on
Fort Parker ten years earlier had become a woman. She was now
the primary wife of a fierce leader of the Indian people. She had
produced at least one male offspring who would be a future Quohadi warrior. She was an accepted member of a powerful, warlike
Comanche tribe.

For the moment, however, Texan energies were turned toward
the enemy to the south. J. Pinckney Henderson, who had recently
been named governor of the new state of Texas, took a leave of absence from his position as chief executive to lead the Texas
Mounted Volunteers into Mexico. The menace posed by the Indians of the South Plains was forgotten in an effort to conquer the
enemy to the south. The Fort Parker massacre, the plight of captives still believed to be among the Indians, and the question of
whether or not Cynthia Ann still lived all passed from public consciousness as Texans girded themselves for battle.

By the mid-1840s, Cynthia Ann's natal family had concluded
that they would never see her again. James W. Parker's statement,
penned in 1844, indicated a belief that she might still be alive. This
however, was little more than an elusive hope. Throughout the
years that Texas remained an independent nation, and for as much
as a decade and a half, this uncertainty about her very existence
continued. It was not until rumors from hunting parties and Indian
agents drifted back to white settlement that there was any reason to
maintain any confidence that she still lived.[4]

John Parker's claim that he made contact with her in an effort
to return her to civilization, if it happened at all, would almost certainly have taken place well after Texas became a part of the
United States. That claim, however, was probably no more than a
bit of bravado.[5]

After the return of the other captives to Anglo civilization, the question of whether a nine-year-old girl could have long survived the rigors of life on the prairie continued to haunt her white relatives.

Rachel Plummer's vivid recollections of her experiences among the Comanches, which were widely read during the years in which Texas remained an independent nation, added intensity to the fears relating to the fate of the young Parker girl. Plummer's accounts, which made references to the severe cruelty she had experienced from her captors, and which described in detail the acts of torture and abuse which she claimed she and others had suffered, only added to their concerns. By 1846 there was serious doubt among most Anglo settlers that the daughter of Silas and Lucy Parker could have survived under such conditions.

With the passage of the years, however, rumors about Cynthia Ann began to surface.

At first these stories were no more than hearsay, for the initial sources of information about her appeared to be of questionable authenticity. Indian traders who were engaged in the nefarious trade of white hostages for substantial rewards could hardly be considered reliable witnesses. Such persons were little respected by either Anglo or Indian. These strange intermediaries between two cultures at war had heard the story around distant campfires of a white girl who had become the wife of a Comanche chief.[6] Considering the sources, their reports were at first taken with little seriousness.

But the tales continued to persist along the frontier.

Contact with Cynthia Ann was made in the early 1840s by one of these traders, a man named either "Stoal" or possibly "Stout." He had been accompanied by a Delaware Indian guide and a Col. Leonard Williams. The trading party was allowed to see her, but when a ransom was offered in her behalf, they were told that all the goods they possessed would not effect her release.[7]

The accounts continued to surface. No longer was it simply the story of a white hostage living among the most violent of the Indians of the South Plains. It soon became the tale of an Anglo woman who was far more than a hostage, who was wed to one of the most powerful and vicious of the Comanche chiefs. The story grew in the telling as it was passed from settlement to settlement: she was described as an Indian princess who, with her war lord husband, in some unexplained way presided over the vast reaches of an unknown empire.[8] In an age of romanticism, even amid the practical realities of the frontier, such a fanciful tale grew in its descriptiveness.

At last there were reports from reliable sources: experienced army officers, thoroughly familiar with life on the prairie, had made contact with the tribe into which Cynthia Ann had been adopted. Capt. R. B. Marcy reported that the captured daughter of the Parker family was, by the end of the 1840s, an accepted member of a nomadic band of Comanches. He stated contact had been made with the tribe of which she was a part, and she had been approached by agents of the United States government. His account concluded with this statement concerning Cynthia Ann: "She could not be persuaded to leave her Indian home."[9]

Marcy personally led an expedition into Indian territory in 1852 for the purpose of impressing the Indians "with the military power and the friendship of the United States."[10] His account of this event, published the following year, indicated that he had hopes of rescuing Cynthia Ann from what he referred to as the "lewd embraces" of the Comanches. However, he reported, he had reliable information that "all . . . she held most dear were with the Indians."[11]

There were other creditable reports relating to the Parker captive. P. M. Butler and M. G. Lewis, Indian commissioners, recounted in their statement to the United States commissioner of Indian affairs that they had made contact with a band of South Plains Indians who held captives. Among them was a "young woman . . . about seventeen years old . . . known as [one of] the Parker children." They declared they had offered the tribe "a large amount of goods and four or five hundred dollars," but "from the influence of her alleged husband, or from her own inclination, she is unwilling to leave the people with whom she associates."[12]

One of the accounts of a contact with Cynthia Ann was later related by a party of hunters who visited an encampment of the Quohadi during one of the more peaceful periods in the ongoing battle between Indian and Anglo while the tribe was camped on the Canadian River. Realizing that the mate of the tribal chieftain was a white, they urged her to return to her birth family. She gave them only an unspoken negative as she pointed to the children at her feet.[13]

Charles Sommer, who, in later years, was a personal friend of Quanah Parker, and who received his information from Cynthia Ann's son, substantiated the account about the mother's repeated refusal to leave the tribe.[14]

One effort to bring her back to her natal family occurred about fifteen years after her capture, when a group of frontiersmen led by Victor M. Ross sought her return to Anglo settlement. She sullenly refused their entreaty.[15]

It was Cynthia Ann's choice to remain on the prairie. In spite of the best efforts of the Parkers, who had offered sizable sums for her return, and military expeditions which had been dispatched for the purpose of effecting her release, she was determined to remain an Indian.

Amid all of the rumors and contradictions, one fact was evident to her white contemporaries: she had been adopted into a nomadic band of Comanches who were known as the Naconi, or the Quohadi.[16] One further fact was now apparent: Cynthia Ann had totally accepted this act of adoption.

Very little was known about this particular band of Indian people. Official reports were even uncertain about the tribal name. These Quohadi were an elusive people. They would appear in one portion of the Comanche range, then dissolve into the sands of West Texas only to reappear at some distant point far from the place where they were believed to be camping. All that government officials could be sure about concerning these nomads was that they were a Comanche tribal sub-culture which was noted both for its warlike tendencies and for an ability to travel great distances ranging over a wide territory.[17]

As more and more reliable information reached her natal family, it became apparent that Cynthia Ann could have left the Quohadi to return to white civilization on any one of several occasions. This, however, she consistently refused to do. Even though she had been snatched from her home in the midst of violence, she had accepted her position among the Comanches. It was a source of continuing amazement for her Anglo contemporaries that she was determined to remain a nomad of the Texas prairie.

There is a record of one final effort to restore Cynthia Ann to Anglo civilization. Capt. R. B. Marcy, who had sought contact with Cynthia Ann two years earlier, returned to West Texas in the summer of 1854 with a company-sized army detachment under his command. This time his unit was commissioned to explore the South Plains and "determine the strength of the Plains Indians."[18]

The Texas legislature had requested that a military expedition into the Comanche heartland be attempted. A detailed account of this trip was later prepared by a member of the troop, W. B. Parker. A primary objective of the manuever was that of seeking clues to the locations of whites who had been taken captive.

Marcy later penned his own record of this journey along with his other experiences in the area and had it published under the title, *The Prairie Traveler*. In this account he discussed the safest ways to travel in Indian territory and described methods of dealing with rattlesnake bites, saddle wounds, and gun accidents. However, he made no mention of any additional contact with the Quohadi, the tribe which he knew was holding Cynthia Ann.[19]

The explorers under Marcy's command left an encampment on the Red River in the summer of 1854, moved westward to the Llano Estacado, saw wolves, buffalo, rattlesnakes and frequent Indian signs, and finally returned to Fort Belknap in the fall. Although Marcy's unit made several peaceful contacts with Comanches, and, on one occasion, "saw Comanche women," there was no mention in either Parker's record or Marcy's account of any further information about Cynthia Ann.[20]

By the time Marcy made his final military exploration of West Texas, Cynthia Ann had become thoroughly acclimated to life on the prairie. By then she considered herself to be a Comanche. She was so completely accepted as a member of the tribe that she no longer stood out as a white captive among Indian people.

She had become one of them.

VIII.

No Word For Home

A heavily loaded wagon train moved slowly across the prairie. This was the Texas Santa Fe Expedition which had left the capital of the republic in early June of the year 1841. By August the adventurers found themselves in the midst of the vast, unbelievable stretches of openness which were the High Plains. For weeks the entourage had struggled with the heavy brush and cross timbers of the country south of the Red River. After two months of torturous travel, the caravan was able to move up from the irregular lands east of the plains and continue at a steady pace across the open country of the prairie.

The expedition included more than 200 men, a caravan of wagons, and a variety of goods intended to be an opening wedge in the establishment of a trade route between Austin and Santa Fe.[1] But the trekkers had not counted on the intensity of the sun, the aridness of the land, or the objections of the native inhabitants of the area. By late August the expedition leadership was faced with two major concerns: locating water sources which were adequate for such a large company of men and animals, and avoiding contact with the Indians who were jealously guarding the scant supply of water which was available in the area.[2]

On August 30 a water search party was surprised by Indians, according to the diary of Peter Gallagher, the primary chronicler of the adventure. Five members of the Texan expedition lost their lives in an ambush by Comanches who were determined to halt the movement of whites into their territory.[3]

Desperately seeking both security and ample water supplies, an expedition scouting party discovered the Palo Duro, a canyon which dramatically bisects the flatness of the plains country. Within its deep recesses flowed one of the tributaries of the Red River. The decision was made to move into the canyon as a refuge from the natives who were attempting to impede their progress. Thinking they would be safe from attack within the canyon, where there was ample water, the travelers laboriously maneuvered their heavily laden wagons down the steep slopes of Palo Duro. This was no easy task in itself, for Charles Goodnight reported that in 1876 it required a half day "to work cattle down the narrow and rugged trail" into the canyon along a route known to have been used by Comanches a few years earlier.[4]

For the Santa Fe-bound Texans, this was a tragic mistake. Unknowingly, they had stumbled into one of the major encampment areas of the Quohadi.[5]

The journeyers soon realized that their every move was being watched. Two days after the main caravan had camped near one of the canyon's major water supplies, the Comanches caused a cattle stampede which cost the travelers eighty-seven animals, which constituted a major source of their food supply.[6]

Goodnight's description of the Palo Duro, when he knew it thirty-five years later, was that of a place in which there was "grass and water in abundance."[7] The Quohadi had no intention of turning this prime area for encampment over to intruders. The white interlopers soon realized that whenever a small group of men ventured away from the main body of the expedition, they were subject to attack.[8]

Under the date September 12, 1841, Peter Gallagher recorded

in his journal the fact that two more members of the exploration party had been killed by the Indians. He then commented in a stoic understatement that the survivors "were dissatisfied."[9]

At last the entourage received word from their advance party which urged them to leave the canyon. This they did with enthusiasm as soon as they could work their way back to the high prairie. They were then able to move rapidly across the level ground of the Llano Estacado, only to be surrounded by a Mexican military force who made them prisoners and marched them off to the dungeons of Mexico.[10]

The Santa Fe Expedition was the first major incursion by white Texans into the heartland of the Comanche. Although it ended in dismal failure, it was nonetheless a harbinger of the intent of Anglo settlers to eventually possess the prairie country. For the natives of the area, this attempt to transect the South Plains was evidence of the determination of an enemy to overrun their territory.

When Cynthia Ann began her quarter century of life on the prairie in the year 1836, the Comanches were in complete control of the South Plains, a domination which they continued to jealously guard.

At some time prior to the year 1690, a migration of these people had taken place. Leaving the territory watered by the Yellowstone and Platte rivers, they had moved south to the Llano Estacado. There they quickly gained control of the extensive prairies and breaks of the area that is today West Texas, eastern New Mexico, and the western portion of Oklahoma.[11]

This was the land of the Comanche. Their unique culture had flourished for nearly two centuries under conditions completely alien to the newcomers who were now beginning to infiltrate the territory between the frontier of Texas settlement and the older native cultures to the west. This was the society of which Cynthia Ann was a part by the time the wheels of the Santa Fe-bound wagons began to roll.

These migrants to the Southwest knew nothing about the area or the people who lived there. Much of the naiveness of the leadership of the Santa Fe Expedition was based on the fact that travelers like Gallagher thought entirely in European terms. For them it was inconceivable that a significant culture could exist under such conditions. It was only when the Anglo settlers learned the secret of the unique nomads' ability to live on the plains that they would eventually be able to displace the Indian from the land he had possessed for generations.

The secret was a simple one. They had learned to utilize the one natural resource upon the arid plains: the herds of buffalo which then roamed the prairies and from which most of the necessities of life came.[12] Even water was carried in containers made from buffalo hide for the long treks across the open prairie between camp sites, a fact which added to their mobility.[13]

Soon after they had migrated to the Southwest, the Plains Indians became excellent horsemen. From a time soon after the introduction of the horse to North America by the Spanish conquerors of Mexico, these nomadic groups were able to move rapidly on the prairie with their mounts. According to one account, "millions of wild horses" were on the Texas prairies at the time the Comanche came to the area.[14]

The tribesmen of the plains captured these animals and used them to their advantage. Much of the success of the Comanche warrior related to his horsemanship. Because of the mobility which the horse gave them, the Comanches were able to establish themselves as the masters of this vast domain, a domination which they maintained well past the middle of the nineteenth century.[15]

This was not only the land of the Indian, but by the 1840s it had become the home of Cynthia Ann.

It was soon after she had reached early maturity and had become a wife of Peta Nocona that her people challenged the Texan expedition as it moved into the heartland of the Comanches. From

this time forward, she was destined to witness the continued interaction between her natal people and her adoptive nation.

W. W. Newcomb, in his study of the Texas Indian, placed the
general locale of the Quohadi as the South Plains near the headwaters of the Red and Peace rivers. This would establish the Palo
Duro, the canyon into which the Santa Fe trekkers had blundered,
as the center of their operations. Other canyons, such as the
Blanco, were places of tribal refuge when on the trail.[16] This was a
vast territory over which the Quohadi moved, camping in a variety
of places to serve as a roving barrier of protection for other tribes in
their demographic grouping.

From the deep walls and recesses of the Palo Duro they were
able to move in various directions, often covering hundreds of miles
in relatively short periods of time.[17]

This area with its unique isolation and rugged canyons, still
today under-populated, was the geographical background for most
of Cynthia Ann's adult life. This was the land to which she would
later desperately seek to return after her life on the prairies had
been abruptly ended by Anglo intervention.

The success of tribes such as the Quohadi in maintaining their
independent existence in this rugged environment is evidenced by
the fact that before the end of the decade of the 1840s, officials in
Washington had become seriously concerned about them. Orlando
Brown, commissioner of Indian affairs, in his report dated November 30, 1849, declared that the "Comanches are the most troublesome of the tribes . . . making captive several women and children."[18]

Soon after the War with Mexico was over, the full force of the
United States Army was brought into the effort to control the natives of the plains. The Indian soon found himself confronted with
an aggressiveness which he had not yet known. The American military, encouraged by an easy victory over Mexico, felt confident it
could soon contain the Apache and the Comanche.

The Forty Year War was about to enter a new phase.

In spite of the confidence born of the conquest of Mexico, the

Anglo soldier, however, could find no Chapultepec to be stormed in his battles on the plains. The enemy was too elusive and too skilled in prairie combat for any quick victory for the white troops. It would be a long and difficult war.

As the warfare between Indian and Anglo escalated during this period, Nocona distinguished himself as a courageous brave. At some point in the 1850s, he would have reached the status of a leading war chief of his people. By the end of that decade, he would be acknowledged as the foremost battle commander of the Comanche nation.

Although his martial leadership made it necessary to spend but little time in camp, it is probable that during these years he took other wives into his lodge. Warriors who did survive the continual contests with the white militia were expected to keep the future potential of the tribe alive by producing as many offspring as possible.

Cynthia Ann accepted these co-inhabitants of her tepee, understanding the practical necessity of polygamy. There is evidence of at least one co-wife in the report of a young girl shot down in the 1860 raid on the Quohadi who obviously was a teenage mate of Nocona.[19] There were certainly others who lived with Cynthia Ann and were sexual partners of her husband. Probably she assisted in the birth and care of the children of her co-wives and tended them as she would her own.

One fact is clear: since she was still producing children until her final year on the prairie, she remained a sexual partner of Nocona and continued to be his principal wife.

Cynthia Ann not only accepted her position among the Indians of the South Plains, but in becoming one of them, she adopted their customs and shared their difficulties and hardships. She experienced both the exhilaration and the tragedies of Comanche life on the prairie.

Her only knowledge of white civilization throughout much of this period would have been from reports by warriors of the tribe who had engaged in battle with the American military. Tales of atrocities by Anglos against Indian tribes would have reached her. Doubtless she knew of Comanche villages attacked by whites, where women and children had been ruthlessly slaughtered. It is conceivable that the violence of the Texan militia against Comanche people at the Council House fight in San Antonio was related to her. She would have had every reason to believe that these events were indicative of the cruelty of the Anglo enemy with which the Plains Indians were at war.[20]

Herman Lehmann, a white youth who was taken hostage at the same age at which Cynthia Ann was captured, "began to regard the Indians as his own people and the whites as his enemies . . . [becoming] indianzied as a result of the brutality by white soldiers against his adopted people."[21] This same process affected the Parker captive, who became absorbed into the culture of her adoptive tribe.

Cynthia Ann, throughout these years, looked and dressed like other members of the Comanche band. Her usual clothing was from the skin of the buffalo, the most common wearing apparel for the people of the plains. On ceremonial occasions, however, she donned buckskin or antelope skin which was sewn and ornamented. She cut her hair and parted it in the middle.[22] The widely published photograph of her holding the infant Topsannah shows her with a hairstyle in keeping with her years upon the prairie.

As the decade of the 1850s neared an end, life became increasingly difficult for the Comanche people. More and more it was obvious that Anglo marksmanship was taking its toll upon the buffalo herds. Hunters were invading the land in increasing numbers and were protected by the growing power of the American military. Tribes such as the Quohadi, who had long been nomads, had even greater movement forced upon them in order to keep up with the constantly decreasing herds of buffalo. During these years, they traveled over vast expanses of land, circling continuously around the Palo Duro area of the South Plains. It became necessary for these people to move over hundreds of miles of prairie as they followed the plains animals which were essential to their existence.

A. E. Butterfield, who wrote about his experiences with the nomadic tribes of the Southwest, stated that their language contained no word for "home." "That," he commented, "was surely true among the Comanches."[23]

Although the language of her adopted people may have contained no word for home, Cynthia had found one in the vast reaches of the plains. She belonged to a tribe that was determined to maintain life upon the prairie as its forebears had done for generations.

IX.

The Turning Point

A band of riders reined in their mounts as they reached the banks of the stream that marked the northern border of Texas. Beyond the river lay Indian territory.

This was late April of the year 1858.

The irregular clumps of mesquite which grew defiantly among the protrusions of rocky soil had just begun to display their greenery. Because of a prolonged winter, the native plant had remained starkly bare; but now, at last, it was putting forth foliage, a sure sign that spring had come. With the coming of the new season, however, once more men were on the move along the frontier.

The war against the Indian was about to resume.

Made up of a few seasoned veterans of the conflict between Texan and Indian, the expedition which stood poised on the banks of the Red River included a number of younger adventurers who were prepared to test their manhood in combat with the dreaded Comanche.

The force was led by a crusty ranger captain named John S. Ford, better known as "Old Rip" for his habit of placing the letters

"R. I. P." beneath his casualty reports. He had been commissioned by the governor of Texas to invade Indian territory and seek out and destroy Indians wherever he could find them.

Ford had set out from Fort Belknap with 102 of the roughest and toughest men available, along with two wagons of military supplies, an ambulance, and a string of pack mules.[1]

Old Rip was too wise an Indian fighter to dare take his men northward without the support of those who knew both the Comanche and the land. He had recruited 113 Tonkawa Indians from the Brazos reservation to assist him in his mission. Traditional enemies of the Comanches, the Tonkawas understood their potential antagonists and were eager to join an effort to bring about their destruction.[2]

The ranger captain held his mount steady as his men reined in beside him. More than a hundred pairs of eyes peered across the vast expanses which lay beyond the modest stream. At last the signal came for which they had been waiting. Tonkawa scouts, who had been ranging over a wide area in company with their white allies, had begun to cross the river. Ford raised his hand: his troop moved eagerly into Indian territory.

The heavily laden wagons which generally accompanied such operations were carefully maneuvered through the uncertain sands of the river bed. At last the pack animals, along with the two cumbersome vehicles, were on the north side of the stream. Neither of these two wagons, however, would return to the soil of Texas.[3]

Moving north of the Red River beyond the protection of military posts in the year 1858 was a risky matter for any white militia. The upper reaches of the river, as well as the land which lay north of that stream, were a part of the vast territory which had long been controlled by the tribesmen of the South Plains.

In reality this was an illegal invasion. Not only was this the homeland of the Comanche, but this was federal territory. Any military action taken north of the Red River was the responsibility of United States Army troops. Ford's rangers were acting solely upon the authority of Governor H. R. Runnels, who had managed to coax funds for the expedition from the Texas legislature for what he had euphemistically called frontier defense.[4]

Several factors had led the governor to commission Ford to undertake this mission. One was the innate fear which most white Texans had of the Indian. Even though the mid-1850s had been a time of relative peace in the area, there was the awareness that as long as Comanches remained in control of the South Plains, there was the possibility they would raid frontier settlements. There was another factor, however, which contributed to the decision to initiate this invasion: additional land was needed for settlement as Anglos continued to establish ranches and farms along the frontier.

Yet another element which argued for the destruction of the Indians of the South Plains was the increasing demand for buffalo pelts, which were bringing good prices in northern and eastern markets. The South Plains still contained vast herds of bison which could easily be slaughtered for profit except for the presence of the Comanche tribes who claimed this area as their own hunting ground.

Added to the financial value of hides was the simple fact, which by this time had become widely recognized in both state and national governmental circles, that the South Plains Indians could not be forced to come to the reservation until the buffalo herds had been destroyed.

Ford's commission was based on a concept of state sovereignty which had little use for federal authority. His authorization for invasion was based upon the flare for self-sufficiency which had marked the history of the Republic of Texas during its years of independence.

The actual wording of Governor Hardin Runnels' commission was quite interesting. The communique to Ford included these words: "I impress on you the necessity of action and energy. Follow any and all trails of hostile or suspected hostile Indians you may discover, and if possible, overtake and chastise them . . . and . . . inflict the most summary punishment."[5]

This was nothing short of open permission to kill and destroy any of the native peoples with whom Ford came in contact. Walter Prescott Webb, in his history of the Texas Rangers, commented on the governor's orders by remarking that he "did not say take prisoners. What he really said was to kill the Indians if you can. The Rangers liked such simple orders."[6]

By May 1, 1858, Ford and his band of frontiersmen and Tonkawas were north of the Red River moving across the grasslands of the area. The Tonkawa scouts believed that at this time of the year they could find the Comanche to the northwest along the Canadian River. The Texan force began a trek in that direction, hoping, with the aid of their Indian allies, to wreak havoc upon their enemy.[7]

By May 10 the scouts had noted the marks of Comanche travois on the land. The next day they reported sighting an encampment of their enemy. Ford's rangers were learning from their allies. In an effort to surprise their adversaries, they began to move with little commotion and made only cold camps.

Early on the morning of May 12, the ranger force crested a rise of ground overlooking a valley of the Canadian River. Before them was a sizable Comanche encampment. The smoke from dozens of campfires rose majestically above the green banks of the river. The Texans were face to face with several hundred of the men, women, and children they were commissioned to destroy.

The element of surprise which Ford had hoped for, however, had been lost. According to one account, the Tonkawas had come across a smaller village of Comanches before their white allies had reached the banks of the Canadian. With ruthless fury the Indian scouts had slaughtered their enemies. Only a single rider had escaped the attack and had made his way to the larger village to sound the alarm.[8]

Another account of the events which led up to the battle at Antelope Hill,[9] which was based, at least in part, on information from Comanche sources, declared that one small Indian encampment on the south bank of the Canadian was overridden by Ford's own men as persons of both sexes and all ages were killed to minimize the possibility of an early warning.[10]

The effort to surprise the enemy was of no avail. As Ford's men prepared to make an assault, they found themselves confronted by a large force of armed and angry warriors. J. W. Wilbarger's account, based on reports from white survivors of the expedition, declared that their antagonists included at least 300 braves.[11] Although reportedly outnumbered, Ford's men, with their rifles and repeating Colt pistols, clearly had the advantage. For a time, however, they halted as they faced the resplendent sight of a Comanche war party prepared for battle.

The Indian force was led by the legendary Pohebits Quasho, a chieftain who maintained his mystique of leadership through a claim that the white man's bullet could not harm him. According to contemporary accounts, he wore a jacket of Spanish mail beneath his battle regalia. This device was an effective defense against the bow and arrow and provided some protection from rifle fire at a distance.[12]

Ford's Tonkawa allies fell back in awe as the Comanche chieftain rode toward them with a full headdress, red flannel streamers, and war paint.[13] Even the well-armed Texans stood their ground nervously as they fingered their weapons and checked their equipment.

What then followed sounds more like a contest of medieval knights preparing for a joust rather than a nineteenth-century battle between frontiersmen and Indians. Quasho rode a spirited steed back and forth along the line of his antagonists as he hurled taunts at them which were clearly understood by both Tonkawa and Texan. At first there was sporadic fire in his direction. His iron jacket appeared impenetrable as several missiles glanced harmlessly off his protective armor. For a time he seemed invincible.

Suddenly, the aura of invulnerability was shattered. One well-aimed bullet struck the fabled chieftain in the neck. He rolled from his mount and lay in motionless death upon the prairie.[14]

At once the rangers charged their enemy, firing at random. Wilbarger, who wrote his account of the battle with a decided anti-Indian prejudice, declared it to be "the grandest assault ever made against the Comanches."[15] In reality it was a bloody slaughter as the firearms of the militia and their Tonkawa allies blasted the life from the braves who were attempting to defend their women and children. Two of Ford's men died, while at least seventy-five Comanches were killed in the vicious contest which followed.[16]

The violent killing continued into midmorning as the rangers and their Tonkawa allies sought out Comanche tribesmen and shot them to death at close range. Finally, the Texans paused in their work of destruction, confident they had put an end to at least one concentration of Comanche strength. Gloating over their success, they began the task of rounding up horses, searching for booty, and taking prisoners. One of those they captured was Quasho's own small son.[17]

But the situation quickly changed. Sul Ross, who had accompanied Ford on the expedition, was credited with first noticing that several hundred Comanche warriors were moving in the direction of the rangers.[18] The new arrivals to the conflict were the Quohadi Comanches who had been camped several miles farther up the Canadian River. Perhaps the scouts of Peta Nocona had learned of the invasion of Ford's troop into the Comanche heartland, and, during reconnaissance on the morning of May 12, heard the sound of rifle fire across the prairie.

Wilbarger declared that "at about one p.m. the rangers looked up and saw about a mile distant a stronger force" than the "four hundred Comanches" they believed they had already routed.[19] Another account, based on reports from the white survivors of the conflict, stated that the Quohadi war chief "came marching with 500 men."[20] Although it is not likely Nocona was in command of such a large war party, for the nearly exhausted Texans, the new arrivals must have appeared to be a vast multitude.

Once again battle lines formed. Ford's Texas militia, side by side with their Tonkawa allies, hastily took up their positions. Facing them in battle array were Nocona's Quohadi warriors.

Wilbarger's account states that the two forces "contemplated each other for an hour."[21] Once again insults were hurled across the lines as Comanche challenged Tonkawa and Texan to hand-to-hand combat.[22] Ford, apparently realizing that his Indian allies felt it was necessary to respond to such challenges, permitted these one-on-one contests of honor to take place. Possibly the battle with Quasho's braves that morning had necessitated the use of so much shot and shell that Ford was doubtful that his men still had enough ammunition to mount an all-out contest against such a sizable force.

After an hour or more of jousting, the man-to-man combat began to give way to general skirmishing. George Hyde reported that "Ford's Indians were getting the worst of it as Comanches usually outdid Tonkawas."[23] General fighting broke out all along the line.

Up to this point all of the extant records of the daylong battle agree. There are conflicting reports, however, of how the battle was concluded.

Wilbarger and DeShields, who received their information from the Anglo accounts of the conflict, claim the battle ended in a victory for the rangers. DeShields stated that once the man-to-man contests had ceased, "a running fight for three or four miles" took place which "necessitated the entire withdrawal of the Indians."[24] Wilbarger declared that "the Comanches at last broke" and "Nocona covered his retreat."[25] However, these two accounts represent only Anglo reports. Sources such as these would never have admitted that a ranger-Indian fight was ever concluded with anything other than a complete victory for the Texans.

Hyde's record of the battle, which he claimed was based on firsthand accounts from both sides (including "many old Indians [who] still remembered the details of the fight" when they were interviewed in 1910), gave a considerably different description of the conclusion of the contest.[26] He declared that the battle "ended in something of a standoff" with the rangers and their allies withdrawing by "marching off before the superior force which faced them."[27]

In all likelihood, the Hyde record is correct. Ford and his militia had given it their best effort. They had decimated one major Indian village and one or two small Comanche camps. They had captured horses and had taken as a trophy of war the fabled coat of mail which had belonged to Quasho.[28] To be able to mount another all-out attack against a large force would have required more ammunition than the rangers still possessed. There was every reason to leave Comanche territory as quickly as possible.

Abandoning their two equipment wagons, they left the scene of the conflict while there was still daylight for the trail southward. To have waited much longer would have been to invite ambush. By midafternoon on May 12, Ford's men began a rapid trek toward the Red River en route to their base camp near Fort Belknap.[29]

Walter Prescott Webb's account of the battle makes no mention of the events of the afternoon after the arrival of the Quohadi. Perhaps, from the ranger standpoint, all of the events of importance took place before Nocona's arrival at Antelope Hill.[30]

Although Ford's white militia later claimed the battle on the Canadian River as a conquest, in a much more realistic sense this was a victory for Nocona, the husband of Cynthia Ann. With his Quohadi braves he had been able to stop the invasion of the white militia and send the intruders back to their home base in near disarray. He had effected a withdrawal of the invading enemy and had accomplished this with little loss of life among his own Quohadi warriors.

In his strategic move toward the white contingent on the afternoon of May 12, Nocona was able to prevent any immediate depredations against the Quohadi, and, at the same time, guarantee the safety of his own people which included Cynthia Ann.

With the death of Quasho and Nocona's final command of the field of conflict, the Quohadi chieftain became a major leader in the Comanche effort to defend Indian territory against white invasion. For the next several years he would be the most feared of the South Plains warriors, the chieftain that every Indian fighter would seek to destroy.

The Battle of Antelope Hill, however, was destined to have a far greater impact upon the future of the Indians of the South Plains than that of determining a principal war chief. It clearly established the fact that the Comanche could no longer hope to maintain absolute domination of the territory which he had long claimed.

Up until this time, the South Plains tribesmen had been little aware of the tremendous forces which existed behind the thin line of frontier settlement. The conflict of 1858 demonstrated the increasing aggressiveness of the whites. While it was, in one sense, a victory for Nocona, it was the beginning of the end for the Comanche people. This single, pitched battle opened the way for Anglo military forces to move deeper and deeper into Indian territory. From this time on, Nocona's Quohadi, along with other Comanche tribes, were forced to go on the defensive. They could do little more than harass their opponents in sudden raids and then flee to the recesses of the canyons still unknown to the white militia. The people Cynthia Ann considered her own would no longer be able to dominate the great expanses of the Staked Plains.

The ranger's newly demonstrated ability to move onto the Llano Estacado prepared the way for the buffalo hunter to come in increasing numbers. With each downed bison, the existence of the Indians on the prairies of the Southwest became more and more precarious as the great herds steadily dwindled.[31] Various estimates have placed the numbers of the South Plains tribesmen in the middle years of the nineteenth century at between 7,000 and 10,000.[32] Even as late as 1868, an official report to President Andrew Johnson on the progress of the control of the Indians of the South Plains stated that there were still 14,800 hostile Comanches and Kiowas with the majority of this general grouping being Comanches.[33]

The success of the efforts of the military to control and exterminate these people is indicated by the fact that Morris Swett, the Fort Sill archivist, reported that by the early part of the twentieth century, no more than 1,171 Comanches had survived. Those who had not died from the onslaughts of the white military had become susceptible to the deadly diseases of those who had forced them to the reservation.[34] The once proud nomads of the plains were destined finally to lose both their traditional hunting grounds and their identity as a people.

Cynthia Ann was well aware of the continuing struggle of her people to maintain control of the prairie. She was knowledgeable of the constant decimation of the buffalo herds. She certainly knew that Peta Nocona was one of the major figures in the Comanche effort to withstand the onslaughts of the Anglo military, and she knew that he was a leader in the desperate attempt to drive back the encroachment of white settlement.

Ford's quasilegal invasion of Indian territory proved one point: it was possible for a white militia to raid the Comanche homeland and escape. For at least two weeks, the Texans, aided by their Tonkawa allies, had operated in land which had long been the absolute domain of the tribesmen of the South Plains.

This was the turning point. This was the beginning of the end for the Comanche. There would now be other invasions, other depredations by whites who were determined to end the very existence of the Indians upon the South Plains.

Within four months, Sul Ross was on another expedition against the native enemy. He sought to destroy a village believed to contain survivors of the raid led by Ford, hoping, as one writer stated it, "to eliminate the Comanches from the Plains."[35]

This time Ross rode with a cavalry force led by Capt. Earl Van Dorn. With four companies of regular troops, the Van Dorn mission managed to surprise an Indian village near the Wichita mountains.[36] Again it was arrows against guns. After the smoke had cleared the white troops were able to count a total of seventy bodies riddled by the fire from their carbines, many of which were those of women.[37] Ross was wounded in this effort, went back to school that fall, and returned to the frontier two years later to resume his role as one of the legendary Indian fighters of the Texas frontier.[38]

The Van Dorn expedition represented a far more powerful force than that of a militia authorized by a state governor. The United States Army, embarrassed by Ford's expedition into Indian territory, was determined to wage an all-out war against the Indians of the Plains. Indian villages continued to be attacked. There was indiscriminate killing, and, in at least one case, the military deliberately attacked a group of Comanches on a peace mission.[39]

The war between Indian and Anglo continued to grow in intensity.

Charles Hummel, a merchant in San Antonio, purchased large quantities of "Colt pistols" and "Navy pistols" in the late 1850s because of what he and his fellow Texans conceived to be the Indian menace. His correspondence with Armand Soubie of New Orleans, his arms supplier, mentioned the fact that four companies of rangers were then stationed in the area because of the fear of Comanche raids.[40]

In early July of 1859, Gen. D. E. Twiggs wrote to General Scott from San Antonio reporting "in this state . . . [there are] a considerable number of Comanche Indians." He proposed vigorous military action on the part of the army so "Texas will be rid of the Comanches."[41] Twiggs followed up his July message with another statement to Scott in September, in which he reported "a family of six persons has been killed on the Rio Grande by Indians."[42] He urged that every effort be made to contain and conquer the South Plains tribesmen.

The recommendations of Twiggs were a part of the army's response to the continued animosity of white settlers toward the Indian. All across the frontier there were demands for action. Even a former Indian agent, John R. Baylor, called upon the authorities for "the removal of all Indians from Texas."[43]

A state of near hysteria was developing among the white settlers. The most peaceful Indian tribes were now suspect. If any horses were missing along the frontier, even in areas where white horse thieves were known to be operating, Indians were blamed.[44] The hysteria reached such a point that on one occasion, U.S. troops were called upon to defend tribesmen of the Brazos reservation who had been staunch allies of the Texans in the war against the Comanches. An army unit had to be mobilized to stop a white mob who carried their distrust of the American natives to the extreme of attempted violence. The situation became so intense that Reservation Superintendent Robert Neighbors sought permission to take his Indian charges out of Texas for their own safety.[45]

Neighbors' name occurs frequently in the extant correspondence of the Office of Indian Affairs. In 1858 he was appointed a special agent with authority to deal with "conditions of the Indian service."[46] In 1859 he was accused of unwarranted "interference" by agents who had been on the field before his arrival. However,

Commissioner I. W. Denver defended Neighbors' right to correct abuses in Texas from his office in Washington, and wrote his special agent declaring he had denied "emphatically that there is any truth in the statements made to you."[47]

Neighbors was one of those who sought to deal both fairly and intelligently with the American natives. Tragically enough, his efforts to quell the anti-Indian hysteria resulted in his death: he was killed by frontier roughs when he made a critical remark about the murder of a harmless Indian.[48]

The extent of this animosity between Texan and Comanche is evidenced by the fact that a transcript of United States hearings regarding Indian land recorded the fact that after the first Comanches had gone on to reservations, Army troops would "sometimes . . . go out to hunt buffalo with them . . . to protect them from Texas Rangers."[49]

In the same year in which the Battle of Antelope Hill was fought, a lanky Midwesterner mounted a platform set on a dusty courthouse square surrounded by the low wooden buildings of a town in central Illinois. It was a site not far from the area where Cynthia Ann had been born. What he said that day would have profound effect not only upon a white nation soon to be divided, but upon the natives of the frontier.

The speaker was Abraham Lincoln.

The occasion was part of the Lincoln-Douglas debates. It was a scene which would be reduplicated repeatedly as the two contestants moved about the state during the months preceding the election to be held that fall. The tall lawyer-politician would lose his bid for a place in the United States Senate to his opponent, Stephen A. Douglas, but, in that series of political discussions, he would establish a position which would influence the American nation for years to come.

"A house divided against itself cannot stand," Lincoln had declared in one of these public statements. "I believe this government cannot endure permanently half slave and half free. I do not expect the Union to be dissolved — I do not expect it will cease to be divided. It will become all one thing, or all the other."[50]

These words, spoken by the man who, two years later, would be elected president of the United States, not only set the stage for the bloody conflict which would be known as the American Civil War, but also proclaimed the hope that the United States could become a single, great nation consisting of citizens of more than one color or race. Lincoln, of course, thought in terms of eventual freedom for the black population of the nation. After he had become president, his statements in Illinois in the summer of 1858 would be cited by Southerners as a reason for secession.

There was another aspect to the Lincolnian dream of a single, undivided nation: this was a concept which would mean freedom for the Negro, but that would require subjugation of the Indian. If the United States was to become one great, united nation stretching from the Atlantic to the Pacific, slavery of blacks might cease, but, in order to produce a united people, freedom for the Red Man upon the plains of the Southwest would be no more.

Those who shared the dream of a united nation spanning all of the territory had given little thought to the situation of the thousands of Indians who still possessed freedom to move about on the lands long claimed by their ancestors. As the push for the end of slavery continued in the north, however, both Northerners and Southerners were agreed, at least, on one issue: the necessity of either controlling or destroying tribes such as those who roamed the South Plains. The Apache, the Kiowa, and certainly the Comanche must be either contained or obliterated. Increasingly, the power of the government of the United States moved toward one of these two ends.

In the same year that Lincoln made his initial call for a nation which would provide freedom for all races, Comanche territory was invaded by Ford's rangers.

It was in these years immediately prior to the American Civil War that South Plains Indians became aware that their area of control was rapidly diminishing due to the military strength of the white settlers. One authority on the history of Indian warfare declared that the late 1850s marked the beginning of the end for the Comanches.[51]

The turning point had been reached.

By the end of the decade, it had been passed.

X.

Sunset on the Prairie

There is unique beauty in a sunset on the plains.

The western sky gradually takes on pastel tints as the sun nears the horizon. The overarching blue, which had been cloudless throughout the day, suddenly accepts fleecy forms capable of reflecting the grandeur of intensified light. Long shadows begin their steady march across the prairie. A landscape which had been drab moments before suddenly reflects vibrant color. Particles of dust which had been languid in late afternoon become shimmering gold.

Then the light is gone.

There is an immediate feeling of coolness which penetrates the plains when there is no sun. It is then that the gathering darkness brings peace.

Cynthia Ann had witnessed countless sunsets during her years upon the prairie. The end of day on May 12, 1858, however, was more than merely the beginning of another night. With the passing of the sun from the sky, there was no peace.

There was only waiting.

Cynthia Ann was one of those who listened in the Quohadi encampment on the Canadian for the sound of warriors returning from the conflict downriver. They knew, in the quiet of the gathering shadows, that the fighting was over. But they had no knowledge of who would return and who would not. As women of the tribe they would wait.

At last there were hoof beats. The sound became sharper as the equine noises echoed along the banks of the stream. Soon the first horsemen were in the camp. One by one the braves entered the open area between the tepees. Each held himself high as he rode. These were not defeated men. It was immediately obvious that the Quohadi warriors had returned once more as victors.

Nocona was not among those who first came to camp. As war chief he stayed behind to ensure that the dreaded whites were completing their withdrawal. He then sent scouts to be certain the invaders were moving directly toward their base and that there would be no feint or countermarch.

At last he came.

He dismounted and allowed Cynthia Ann to take his horse to be tethered. He entered his tepee.

With the coming of the first light of day on May 13, once again Nocona returned with his war party to the scene of the battle. He waited there until there was further confirmation that the Anglos were returning rapidly to their own land. The Quohadi scouts had done their work well, trailing after the departing rangers and their Tonkawa allies.

In the meantime, an effort was made to succor the followers of the fallen Quasho who had survived the attack. Nocona's presence in the area gave the defeated tribal members who had fled into the isolated draws and brushy areas a chance to return. Scaffolds were erected to hold the bodies of those who had been slaughtered by the whites. The personal possessions of the dead were placed beside them to ensure that their needs would be met in the afterlife.[1]

After order had been brought from the chaos of destruction, the remnants of Quasho's band moved from the scene of conflict and left the elevated bodies of their dead to the elements. Their movement was to the east, for the Van Dorn expedition, four months later, reported that they found this tribal remnant in the Wichitas when United States Army troopers continued their war against the Indian.[2]

The Quohadi moved to the west, for the buffalo would have been plentiful upon the high plains at this time of year. With the warmth of an early summer sun, it was necessary to seek out the animals that made existence possible in this semidesert land.

Life resumed for both Comanche bands as each continued to follow the centuries-old customs of their people.

Nocona spent no time gloating over his success in expelling the whites from Indian territory. He knew that the enemy would soon return. Cynthia Ann shared this knowledge. Once the enemy had entered their heartland, the Comanches were aware they would come again. There would be others, many others, who would enter their territory.

Each time they came there would be death.

No member of the tribe spoke of such things, for it is not the way of the Indian to dwell upon tragedy or potential destruction. People such as the Comanche had learned to exist in the fullness of the moment without granting permission for dread to overwhelm them. They had developed the ability to live in sunshine on the prairie, even when its light was fading from the sky.

This was a unique form of existentialism: each day, each hour, even each moment was a time within itself, an opportunity to be in tune with the warmth of the sun and the light of each day without fearing what would come with the sunset.

Cynthia Ann had adopted this concept. She knew that there were difficult times ahead for her people. But she was determined to live among them without dread of what lay beyond the setting sun.

The Quohadi reacted to the event of May 12 by continuing their nomadic movement. This was their best defense. Back they went to the high plains, where the buffalo were still plentiful. There would be warm, fresh meat for the eating, new robes and clothing to replace apparel which had become unusable. There would be replenishment for skins upon the tepees which had been weakened by the snows of winter.

With the fullness of spring, again the travois would move across the prairie. Camp after camp would be made and then remade.

The Quohadi knew that mobility was essential to their defense. The fact that the rangers had come deep into their territory had made it clear that their invulnerability was no more.

These final years were increasingly difficult for Cynthia Ann as she shared the intensified hardships of her adopted people. Their very survival spoke well for their tremendous resilience.

One of the factors which made it possible for them to continue in these sunset years was that of their intense spirituality. Religion was a significant part of Indian culture. It was a holistic faith which blended ritual, magic, and health and played an important role in tribal survival.[3]

Cynthia Ann adopted the beliefs and practices of her people. She was able to meld her Parker fundamentalist Christianity with the primitive spiritualism of the Indian.[4] Reared in the vigorous theological atmosphere of her natal family, which would have demanded a considerable knowledge of the scriptures of the Old and New Testaments, she was able to relate this basic religiosity to the primitive spirituality of the Comanche.

Ole Nystel, in his two autobiographical accounts, described his religious development as a captive of the South Plains Indians. His experiences would have paralleled those of Cynthia Ann, since he attributed his own survival to his ability to relate his Christian convictions to the Indian belief in a Great Spirit.[5] Cynthia Ann's captivity at the very age in which religious consciousness generally appears,[6] would have forced her to blend her childhood teachings with the spirituality of her captors. Perhaps, in this, she found her major solace during these increasingly tragic sunset years.

The religious observances of her tribe which she practiced included the sacramental use of peyote. Her son, Quanah, would later perpetuate the use of this drug as a support for the spiritual consciousness of the Comanches on reservation, insisting that such practices had been handed down from his ancestors.[7] The United States government later recognized the validity of these rites and has continued to license the ritualistic use of peyote by the descendants of the Indians of the Southwest.[8]

Sanapia, a medicine woman who was associated with Quanah in his efforts to revive traditional Indian religious rites on the reservation, was considered the "last surviving Comanche Eagle doctor."[9] She claimed a "Christian father" and a mother who was a "traditional peyotist." She believed in the curative powers of the drug which "can aid in healing any type of human affliction." Peyote was used ritually when inhaled, and "dried peyote buttons [were] used to make a tea" which was also used as a painkiller. In addition to her use of the drug both ritually and for healing purposes, Sanapia also affirmed her confidence in the efficacy of "cedar smoke . . . when fanned over a person [or] to wash out a house . . . when sad."[10]

The seeking of visions was important to the Comanche, particularly in times of crisis or discouragement. One authority on the culture of the Plains Indians described the practice of the quest for visions: the seeker would dress only in moccasins and a breechclout and climb to the top of an isolated hill. On the way there would be four stops, a sacred number for the Comanches. The vision seeker would pray at each pause. When a lonely spot had been reached, spiritual petition would continue through the night with the supplicant facing east. This could continue for four days of fasting, during which time a vision was expected to come.[11]

Although such prolonged seeking for religious experience was probably practiced more by male leaders of the tribe than by the women who had day-to-day responsibilities, Cynthia Ann was aware of such rites. It is probable that she took part in similar activities. This would be a means of sustaining her own inner being in the midst of a people who had a deep spiritual consciousness. Religious practices were essential for the Quohadi named Parker as she sought to find confidence and strength in the waning days of the power of the South Plains people.

One aspect of spirituality among the natives which could have had a negative effect on Cynthia Ann was that of the infiltration of the Ghost Dance religion into the region. This came late to the South Plains, but there is no doubt that it reached the area. This was a type of religiosity which had been manifest earlier in the century among the northern tribes. An Indian prophet, who used the name Isatai, introduced this faith to the Comanches claiming this practice was a means of defeating the Anglos and saving the buffalo herds.[12]

One portion of the Ghost Dance concept was the belief, at least among some of the northern tribes during the nineteenth century, that all whites must be destroyed. Those who had become a part of the Indian people were to be purged from the tribe by death. A person judged to be an enemy, either male or female, according to one account, would be sacrificed to the god Tirawa. This was done in a particularly cruel fashion: the victim would be tied to elevated cross poles, then shot with arrows but without inflicting mortal wounds. The arrows then would be painfully removed before a final point of flint was forced into the breast. The body of the sacrificed person would then be burned as an act of atonement.[13]

Although there is no record of such an event having taken place among the South Plains tribes, it is possible that Cynthia Ann was aware of similar practices of the Ghost Dance religion when it began to spread to the southern prairies.[14] Her position as wife of a powerful war chief and the mother of Comanche children, however, would have prevented any suggestion that she might be considered a potential sacrificial victim. Her security also rested upon her complete acceptance by the Quohadi and her total allegiance to Comanche culture.

Cynthia Ann continued, during the sunset years, as a secure and respected member of the tribe, maintaining a loyalty to her adopted people. Peta Nocona not only guaranteed her protection, but continued to maintain sexual relations with her as his wife.

Less than two years after the Battle of Antelope Hill, Cynthia Ann gave birth to her last child. This was a girl who, unlike Cynthia Ann's two living sons, would not be expected to go to some distant prairie to die at the hands of the hated white enemy. This was the child Topsannah, the flower of the prairie,[15] a single moment of beauty in an increasingly desolate situation.

Topsannah's birth must have taken place early in 1860, since she was an infant in her mother's arms when Cynthia Ann was returned to white civilization in December of that year. This fact would indicate not only that Nocona continued to relate to her sexually, but that she remained the principal wife of the Quohadi war chief throughout her years upon the prairie.

There is the possibility of another female birth prior to that of Topsannah. Quanah, late in life, referred to the raid which resulted in the capture of Cynthia Ann by stating "In that fight they captured my mother, two sisters, my brother . . . I escaped."[16] More than likely his reference to an older sister was based on the fact he would have considered the young woman who was in the lodge of Nocona, when the tribe was surprised by the whites, as a sibling rather than a younger wife of his father.

It was about this time, either during her pregnancy or immediately after the birth of Topsannah, that a personal servant was assigned to Cynthia Ann. Documents in the Fort Sill Archives refer to a Mexican slave who became her bodyguard.[17] One source gave him the name "Yaqua" and stated that he "frequently commanded hunting parties."[18]

Peta Nocona accepted the full responsibility of defending his people from the continued infiltration of the Anglo enemy. Since the events of 1858 had thrust him into the position of a major war chief of the South Plains Indians, it was necessary in the final days of the 1850s for him to lead raids against the steady encroachment of white settlement.

On one of the Comanche forays believed to have been led by Nocona, a family of settlers named Sherman were attacked in 1860 at their frontier home on the western edge of Parker County. The father and two children managed to escape, but the mother of the family, who was pregnant, was wounded. It was reported she died the next day after giving birth to a dead baby.[19]

A public gathering of angry settlers was convened in Weatherford, Texas, immediately after the attack. The area inhabitants called for the death of all Indians. Weapons which were reported to have been used by Comanches were displayed, and scalps were shown. It was claimed by the promoters of the assembly that these scalps had been taken from Anglos. One of these was said to have been that of a young, white woman. "Exterminate the Indians" was the theme of the gathering.[20] Anglo hysteria reached such an intense level that rangers and members of the militia were urged to kill all of the nomads of the Plains in retaliation.

Comanche leaders such as Peta Nocona knew that counterattacks would come with increasing severity. The assignment of a personal bodyguard to Cynthia Ann and her youngest child was an effort to provide security as the Forty Year War reached a new level of intensity. This was a shield of protection which might have been successful, at least for a time, had it not been for a December sandstorm and an unrelenting white militia led by one of the men who had been present at the Battle of Antelope Hill.

Sunset on the prairie was rapidly approaching for the Comanches of the plains.

For Cynthia Ann it would come even sooner than for the other members of the tribe.

XI.

The Recapture

By the fall of 1860, Sul Ross had become known for his exploits as an Indian fighter. It was then that he entered the territory of the enemy once again, this time as the captain of a ranger company.

The autumn had been mild and his expedition had been able to move with little difficulty across the expanses of the upward sloping lands which spread westward from the Texas frontier. As mid-December approached, however, the inevitable happened. A series of northers began a march down from the high country to the broken lands east of the plains, bringing with them the bitter chill of winter. It was a time in which most military expeditions were content to seek the shelter of the barracks within a walled enclosure.

Ross was a determined antagonist. So far, in his latest efforts to seek out the Comanche, he had seen few Indian signs. It was not in his nature to be content to return to the relative comfort of a military post without having taken part in a serious engagement in the continuing war between Anglos and natives of the plains.

The ranger force was augmented by a detachment of troops

from the Second Cavalry along with a band of frontiersmen from Bosque County. Their mission was that of locating and destroying Ross' old antagonist, Peta Nocona.

The ranger captain was not alone in this quest, for the husband of Cynthia Ann had become the most feared of all the South Plains tribesmen. The wily chief had successfully evaded both the military forces and the various militias which had been attempting his destruction. He and his Quohadi warriors had been highly effective in their elusive hit-and-run tactics as they sought to hold back the continued infiltration of white settlers into the land of the Comanche. For this reason there was renewed Anglo determination to bring about his annihilation.

Following a trail near the Pease River, Ross suddenly came upon Comanches preparing to break camp. The accounts from Ross' men indicated that the encampment was a large one.

The latest December norther had begun its sweep through the area. Swirling sand from the storm obscured the scene, preventing the prey from hearing or sensing the approach of a predator. Realizing the advantage he had, Ross gave the command to attack. The Indians, taken completely by surprise, broke and ran in all directions. Ross and one of his aides, Tom Killiheir, believed they saw Nocona mount and flee, followed by another figure on horseback. Pursuing the fleeing forms up a shallow draw through the blinding storm, Ross shot a young Indian girl who had been riding with the Comanche they thought was Nocona. She was blown from her horse and lay dead upon the path.

Both Ross and Killiheir continued to fire. One of their bullets struck the antagonist they believed to be the tribal chief. He fell to the ground.

As the injured man lay dying, he was still able to direct well-aimed arrows toward the attackers. A shot from Ross' pistol finally broke the arm of the downed man, rendering him helpless. As pelting sand and howling wind added to the confusion, a shot was fired that ended his defiance. One account of this shooting declared that the dying man pulled himself upright and sang a Comanche death song before he slumped to the ground.[1]

Ross believed that in this encounter he had killed Peta Nocona. For years after the brief conflict, Anglo accounts of the battle gave Ross credit for ending the career of one of the most elusive of the Comanche war chiefs. However, it was Quanah Parker, the son of Nocona and Cynthia Ann, who later insisted that his father had survived the raid.[2] Charles Goodnight, in his later years, dictated a statement to historian J. Evetts Haley declaring emphatically: "Nocona was not there at the time . . . he lived many years afterwards."[3]

Apparently, either Peta Nocona was not present at the time of the 1860 raid on the Quohadi or the wily chief was able to disappear into the raging sands of the storm to fight again. There is evidence that Nocona was involved in an encounter with a band of rangers who claimed they killed him in 1861.[4]

Obviously, more than one group of Indian fighters sought the honor of having dispatched Peta Nocona. Perhaps the mantle of Pohebits Quasho, who had claimed that Anglo firepower could do him no harm, had fallen upon him. At least for the moment, he seemed immune to the effectiveness of the bullets of his white enemies.

Some modern writers have insisted that neither Nocona nor any of his warriors were present at the time of the attack.[5] It is quite likely that Nocona was not in the encampment at the time of the raid, and, in the confusion, no significant response to the surprise attack was possible. In any case the Quohadi were caught by surprise, and Nocona, and at least some of his braves, were either absent or able to escape the ranger onslaught.[6]

After Ross' men had gunned down the defender they believed to be Nocona, almost certainly the Mexican slave Yaqua, they turned their attention toward other possible opponents.[7] Nearby they saw a mounted figure through the swirling sands of the storm. They were about to open fire when they discovered that the Indian on horseback was holding an infant.

Looking into the face of his captive, Ross suddenly exclaimed to Killiheir, "This is a white woman!"[8]

Ross later stated he immediately suspected that this was Cynthia Ann Parker. Her appearance was that of an Indian: her skin tint had become bronzed by a quarter of a century of sunshine on the prairie. Her hair and clothing styles were those of the Comanche.

Her identity became more obvious after the successful raiders had camped on a creek some miles distant from the scene of the recapture. She was recognized as a white because of the fact that in the darkness of night by the campfire, an officer heard a woman crying, which seemed unusual. He reported, "No Indian woman gives way to her feelings."[9] He, too, suspected that the new captive was Cynthia Ann.

Ross' forces did not tarry long at the scene of their victory. Realizing they were still dangerously deep in Indian territory, the rangers quickly retreated to their base camp which had been established at Camp Cooper, a frontier outpost near Fort Griffin on the Clear Fork of the Brazos.[10]

Like his father, Quanah was either not present during the raid or was able to make good his escape from the Peace River conflict. He was at least fourteen years old at the time. He continued to live with his father and his brother, Pecos, as members of the Quohadi remnant. The older son eventually took his place as a tribal leader.[11]

Cynthia Ann, still holding her infant, was led back to the ranger base of operations. Once more she had become a military trophy of conquest.

At first her major concern was for the safety of the infant she was carrying in her arms. She would tell her captors nothing. In time, however, she accepted the statements made by those who had taken her prisoner that her husband, Peta Nocona, had been killed in the battle. She was then led, with considerable reluctance, back toward white society.

Her nearest known relative, Isaac Parker, then a state senator, was notified soon after the rangers returned to their post.[12] He made the journey to Camp Cooper to claim her, taking her to his home near Birdville, a few miles east of Fort Worth.[13]

Senator Parker,[14] who was an older brother of Cynthia's father, found a place for her in his Birdville residence and made efforts to wean her back to an acceptance of Anglo civilization.

During the early days of her return to her natal people, Cynthia Ann gave little information to those she considered to be her captors.[15] According to one account, however, when her childhood name was mentioned in her presence, she would place her hand over her breast and say simply: "Cynthia Ann, me . . . me . . . me!"[16]

News of her recapture spread quickly.

The fact she had lived for years as a Comanche and the legends which surrounded her were widely known. Isaac Parker arranged for her to travel to the state capital, where she was viewed as an object of curiosity. She was present in the Senate chamber during the Secession Convention in Austin, having been taken there by a family friend. This was an experience which she found to be most unpleasant. Unaware of the reasons for the rancor of those present at the political gathering, and aware that many eyes were focused upon her, she believed she was under judgment.[17]

The legislature finished its political proceedings but found time to grant her a pension.[18] The effort to reacclimate her to Anglo society had begun.

For the thoroughly Indianized Cynthia Ann, however, there was great reluctance to accept any of the trappings of her natal culture. She would sleep only on the floor. On more than one occasion, she mounted a horse and attempted to escape from her relatives, whom she considered to be her captors. A Parker family source stated "for a long time she had to be watched very closely, for she took every opportunity to try to get away."[19]

During her stay in Birdville, she was taken to nearby Fort Worth, where a photograph was made of her and her infant child, Topsannah.[20]

Since it was obvious that she would not accept life in the home of Isaac Parker, and possibly since Birdville was dangerously close to the frontier, plans were made to transfer her to the home of relatives living in East Texas. After a year with her uncle, she and her child were moved to the residence of her brother, Silas Mercer Parker, Jr., who was then living in Van Zandt County.[21]

Her removal from Birdville to a location seventy-five miles to the east was an effort to take from her any opportunity for a successful escape attempt. On January 8, 1862, only a little more than twelve months after Ross' raiders had captured Cynthia Ann, Silas Mercer Parker, Jr., was appointed her legal guardian.[22] He took her into his home in Van Zandt County in another effort to woo her back to an acceptance of her natal culture. She entered into her stay in her new location with stoic resignation. It was apparent, however, that she did not accept her brother as a kinsman and lived in his home with her daughter as unwilling prisoners.

There was little communication during this period between Cynthia Ann and those who were seeking her restoration to Anglo civilization.[23] Coho Smith, a Confederate agent who, soon after the beginning of the Civil War, was seeking to establish contacts with Mexican traders in Texas for his government, visited in the Van Zandt County residence. He later reported being a guest of the Parkers for a meal at which Cynthia Ann was present. Knowing a little of the Comanche language, he sought to make conversation with her, whereupon she sprang up, knocking dishes off the table as she asked to be taken away from Anglo settlement and allowed to return to the Quohadi.

"Mi corazón está llorando todo el tiempo por mis dos hijos," she cried out in Spanish, a language which she had learned during her prairie years. Smith reported that she pled with him to do whatever was necessary to help her return to her Comanche people, whom, she assured him, "will be so glad if you bring me to them they will give you anything I would ask of them."[24]

Smith had difficulty in explaining why he could not agree to her request, even though he talked with her again the next day before leaving the Parker farm to resume his work.[25]

This event would indicate that even in this period, well over a year after her recapture, Cynthia Ann was far from willing to accept her position as an Anglo citizen of Texas.

One more effort was made to find a place where she might be

able to adjust to life in white society. She was transferred to the home of the Ruff O'Quinns, her sister and brother-in-law, in Anderson County, a location which was even farther from the frontier.[26] This final effort to effect her reculturing took place about 1863. Again, this was probably a Parker family decision which represented another attempt to de-Indianize the recaptured woman.

It was during these months that Cynthia Ann began to communicate with her white relatives. One record indicated that she was able "to relearn the English language."[27] Although she regained some use of her natal tongue, she never found her place among her well-meaning Anglo kin.

In spite of all of the efforts of the family to wean Cynthia Ann back to a full acceptance of Anglo civilization, she continued to grieve for the loss of the life she had lived for a quarter of a century. Sadness was deepened for her when the infant, Topsannah, whom she had saved from the Ross raid, died of a fever.[28]

This tragedy overwhelmed her.

Topsannah had been her last link to the life she had lived as an Indian. From that time forward, she withdrew within herself. The potential for communication which had been gradually developing between her and her white relatives came to a halt, and she returned to an attitude of withdrawal into lonely, self-imposed solitude. One of the more extensive accounts of Cynthia Ann's final days, a privately published paper which represents tradition within the Parker family, summed up this period with these plaintive words: "She sat and sang her song of grief and lashed her breast."[29]

The cutting of her breasts was an expression of her sorrow, an act which was inconceivable to her white family. The severe lashing of this portion of her body symbolized her conviction that she had no reason to give life or to continue to live. This act was in keeping with her Indian experience; symbolic acts, particularly those which involved self-inflicted pain, had deep significance. One authority on Comanche culture commented that mourning was generally "accomplished by self mutilation," which was a declaration that "they were not afraid of death."[30]

In Cynthia Ann's case, this act meant even more: it was a final declaration of her rejection of the Anglo society which was about to complete the destruction of the people she had made her own.

After the loss of Topsannah, Cynthia Ann's health continued to decline. She died in 1864, grieving until the last for the existence from which she had been removed — a victim of the long and bitter struggle between Anglo and Indian for the control of Texas.[31]

XII.

Tightening the Noose

The war on the frontier would continue for a full decade after the death of Cynthia Ann. In the same year in which she died, it is probable that Peta Nocona, her war chief mate, also met death.[1]

By this time the Quohadi had become a remnant tribe only able to exist by employing the skillfully elusive tactics of the nomad.

The Comanches were no longer the lords of the South Plains.

The fact that a small band of rangers could successfully attack a Quohadi encampment in 1860 and capture a chieftain's wife was one more piece of evidence that the Indian had lost control of the southern prairies.

Two decades earlier, in the year 1840, about the time Cynthia Ann became a mate of Peta Nocona, Comanche leaders met with the chieftains of the Arapahos, the Cheyennes, and the Kiowas. That gathering produced a mutual defense pact designed to withstand the continuing encroachment of Anglo settlement. This was the same year in which the Council House fight took place in San Antonio, an event which convinced many Indian leaders that whites could not be trusted.[2] From that time forward, the South Plains natives were determined to resist with every means possible the increasing hordes of settlers who were entering Texas.

The Comanches were then at the peak of their power, numbering their people in the thousands. Because of their mobility and their fierce warlike qualities, they were able to continue, at least for a time, to dominate the southern plains.[3]

The 1840 pact was a change of direction for the Comanches who had long sought to control this vast land for their own people. These South Plains tribesmen, along with their allies, were prepared to turn their martial energies toward a common foe, the white man. This was the initial stage of the Forty Year War, which raged throughout Cynthia Ann's adult years.

After the expulsion of the Cherokees from East Texas, the Council House fight, and the raids and counter raids which followed those events, both Indian and Anglo demonstrated an increasing determination to withstand what each believed to be the onslaughts of the other.

In many instances, raids by Comanches on white settlers were answered by Texan attacks on Indian villages. Women and children were ruthlessly slaughtered. Because of the Anglo inability to distinguish between the various tribal groups, depredations were carried out on native communities which had never been involved in the launching of raiding parties.

Both sides committed atrocities in the desperate contest for the control of the frontier.

During the years in which Texas maintained its independence, only limited funds were available for offensive action against the Indian. The ongoing war necessitated the building of many small, family, or community forts similar to the one built by the Parkers. Bird's Fort, established in 1840 near Fort Worth,[4] was but one of many isolated fortifications which came into being on the frontier. One can well imagine that gates to such structures were no longer left open as they had been at Fort Parker when there was any possibility of the approach of Indians.

Even though these forts were primarily defensive establishments, the very fact that they existed in land long controlled by the Indian appeared to the natives of Texas as acts of aggression. Each fortification was one more defiant thrust toward Comanche territory.

Other than the building of forts, however, the Texans had only limited means of continuing the war. The government of the Republic of Texas could do very little to assist in the security of its frontier. It had overextended itself financially in the Cherokee War. Lacking both funds and manpower for extensive operations against the Indian, the settlers had to content themselves with occasional counter raids in the ongoing battle.

Immediately after Texas became a part of the United States, however, a victorious military was able to turn its attention toward the elimination of the natives from the South Plains.

It now became national policy to encircle the elusive nomads in an effort to drive them to a reservation where they could be disciplined and supervised by the army. The battle plan was a simple one: a circle of well-staffed military forts would be built around Comanche territory. This noose would be gradually tightened until the South Plains tribesmen were either brought under control or completely destroyed.

With the increased financial backing of the government in Washington, the building of strong frontier posts was possible. Construction began on a line of major military establishments: Fort Inge, built in 1846 west of San Antonio; Fort Bliss and Fort McIntosh, erected on the Rio Grande in 1849; Fort Belknap, constructed in 1851 on the Brazos River; Fort Clark in 1852 near Del Rio; and Fort Griffin in the mid-1850s.[5]

The years which followed the recapture of Cynthia Ann gave the South Plains nomads some respite as military strength which had been amassed in the Southwest was withdrawn to fight America's Civil War. After the cessation of hostilities in the east, however, the strategy of fort building continued until the Comanche domain was completely surrounded.

Fort Sill was built immediately north of the Red River, and Fort Richardson to the south of the river, protecting settlement in

North Texas. San Antonio became a military headquarters with a fort named for Sam Houston, the very Texan who had sought to establish peaceful relations with the Indian. In the Big Bend country, the isolated soldiers stationed at the pre-Civil War military establishment of Fort Davis were given the responsibility of protecting westward moving settlers who chose a southern route of travel. Other important outposts had been built to the east: Fort Stockton and Fort Lancaster.[6]

From these lonely posts, cavalry soldiers were able to do far more than provide protection for those who sought refuge within the walls of their fortifications. They were able to range over thousands of square miles of territory as they steadily narrowed the domain of the Indian.

Large numbers of recruits, many of whom were blacks, were sent into the isolated expanses of Southwest Texas and the territory of New Mexico to subjugate the Comanche. The Indian found the blacks to be able antagonists, giving them the name "buffalo soldiers." The term was believed to have come from the resemblance which the Indians saw between the black soldier's hair and the buffalo's shaggy coat. By naming their opponents for an animal which was considered of such great importance in Indian culture, however, they honored their foes by linking them with the valued buffalo.[7]

At first the Indian had the upper hand in the contest in the Southwest since he knew the land far better than the recruits sent against him. As the Anglo military forces became more adept at Indian warfare, the tide turned against the Comanche and their allied tribes. The turning of the tide was only possible because of the effectiveness of courageous black troops who were determined to prove their prowess against a relentless foe.

The buffalo soldier became an increasingly able Indian fighter. Not only did he possess considerable courage, but he was able to withstand the hardships of the trail and the difficulties occasioned by the conditions of life in a semidesert climate. It is one of the equivocal facts of history that black soldiers were an important factor in winning the West for the whites.

The encircling noose of military power which now surrounded the nomads of the plains continued northward from El Paso through the territory of New Mexico. Posts such as Fort Craig, Fort Stanton, Fort Marcy, and Fort Union had been established there. These major forts were supported by lesser outposts as the ring of steel sought not only to encircle the Comanche, but to cut him off from possible alliance with other Indian groups.

Col. R. B. Marcy, who himself had had extensive contact with the Plains Indians, recommended in these final days of conflict that the entire Bureau of Indian Affairs be removed from the control of the Department of the Interior in Washington and be placed under the authority of the War Department.[8] Although there is no evidence that serious consideration was given to this bureaucratic change, there was little need for such an action.

The army was soon in complete charge of the situation on the frontier.

Military detachments were stationed in the Department of Missouri. Fort Lyon was built on the upper reaches of the Arkansas River; Fort Dodge and Fort Larned were located farther to the east on the same tributary. The circle was supported by other forts to the north: Fort Wallace, Fort Hays, Fort Harker, and Fort Riley.[9]

The circle was reduced until the natives of the plains had no direction in which to go other than that of accepting life on the reservation. The alternatives became increasingly clear: death in battle for the warrior and starvation for the women and children of the tribe.

The last years of Indian warfare were tragic ones as the remnants of the once powerful Comanche people were driven further and further into the recesses of the badlands of West Texas.

Troopers were finally able to dominate the entire southern plains. Even the isolated lands around the Palo Duro and Blanco canyons, which had been havens for the Quohadi during the years Cynthia Ann lived upon the prairie, ceased to be places of security for the Comanche remnant. The soldier was able to capture both goods and horses from the embattled Indians. Without access to the buffalo herds, which were rapidly decreasing before the steady invasion of the white hunter, the Comanche could no longer recoup his losses or sustain life on the prairie.[10]

One last desperate effort was made by the remnants of the South Plains natives. Isatai, a charismatic Indian leader, gathered together the Comanche tribes who had not accepted the 1867 Medicine Lodge Treaty for a final attempt to expel the Anglo from the plains. Their primary target was a well-armed band of buffalo hunters headquartered in an encampment on the Canadian River known as Adobe Walls.[11]

It was in this battle that the son of Cynthia Ann was to play a major role in the final effort to drive the hated hunter from the area. But when the last battle for the South Plains was over, no longer was there a place for the Comanche on the prairie. The buffalo hunter's gun not only eliminated the source of food and shelter for these people, but it brought a conclusive end to their hope for survival on the plains.[12]

It is significant that it was Quanah who was one of those who held out until the end of the third quarter of the nineteenth century. He would then become influential in leading a broken people to accept an existence among his white ancestors.

Cynthia Ann had lived in a culture which was destined for extinction. It was after her forced return to white civilization that the final destruction of her people began. As the noose tightened, perhaps, in some ways, it was well that Cynthia Ann had been snatched from her adoptive people before the end was obvious. It would be left to her son to witness the final and complete end of Indian power on the prairies of the Southwest.

XIII.

The Reunion

The frontier post of Fort Sill stood defiantly on the edge of Indian territory. Built to drive a destructive wedge into the dwindling power of the Comanche, lookouts could peer from the security of their stone structures toward the west. From there they could easily observe the approach of a potential enemy across the grasslands which stretched to the horizon and beyond. Officers on duty could only hope that the cloud of dust in the distance was one generated by another band of Indians coming to the post to lay down their weapons in surrender.

In the years which followed the American Civil War, with the full force of the military might of the United States turned toward the Indian, and the herds of buffalo continually being destroyed, one by one various tribes came submissively to the reservation. There were Plains Indians, however, who continued to defy the entreaties of the Indian commissioners and the threats of the horse soldiers from Fort Sill.

One of these bands was led by the son of Cynthia Ann. Having learned the wiles of plains warfare from his father, Peta Nocona,

Quanah Parker held out until the beginning of the last quarter of the century. But for his tribe, the end had really come in 1860.

Whatever impact the Sul Ross raid on the Quohadi encampment at Pease River may have had upon the tribe, at least one fact was clear: the rangers succeeded in capturing the wife of a chieftain, Cynthia Ann.

Even if Sul Ross was wrong in his belief he had killed the war chief of the Quohadi, there was certainly no doubt that the son of the chief, Quanah, had survived. Since he had been born about 1845, he would have been approaching maturity at the time of the Ross attack.[1] In the years which followed the raid, he matured to full manhood and took an increasing role of leadership among the embattled Comanche remnant.[2]

Quanah later made reference to his upbringing in a speech he delivered to an Anglo audience in July 1896: "My mother raised me like your mothers raised their children, but my father taught me to be brave and learn to fight to become chief of my people."[3]

In 1867 he was present at an intertribal council on the Nescatunga River when various bands of Comanches, Kiowas, Arapahos, and others gathered to confer with representatives of the United States government who were then seeking to put an end to the Indian war on the South Plains. The Medicine Lodge Treaty, which resulted from this gathering, brought the majority of the conferring tribes to the reservation.[4]

Quanah was among those who did not accept the provisions of the treaty. For the next seven years, he participated in the efforts of the surviving Comanches to maintain their independence in the rugged lands of West Texas. Because of their knowledge of the area, this determined remnant of the Quohadi were able to take advantage of the break country which separates the High Plains from the gently rolling farm and ranch lands of Central Texas. It was there they made their headquarters as they continued to resist the efforts of the United States military to bring them onto a reservation.[5]

Robert Goldthwaite Carter, in his recollections published in 1919, recorded his own experiences as an officer serving under Gen. R. S. Mackenzie in the war against the Indians. He placed the center of operations for the Quohadi during these final days of the Forty Year War as that of the Blanco Canyon area. He described this as "northwestern Texas, the so called panhandle . . . [which] extends through parts of three counties — Crosby, Floyd and Hale." He reported that White River, which flows through the canyon, was sometimes known as "Catfish Creek." It was there, he declared, that "there had dwelt for many years a nomadic band of savages, known as Qua-ha-da Comanches."[6]

From the broken lands of the Blanco Canyon and the other isolated draws and recesses of the area, the Comanche remnant was able to move as far south as Fort Stockton or ride rapidly into the neighborhood of Gainesville; or, at other times, appear unexpectedly at Fort Richardson, strike quickly, and then return to lands little known to the cavalryman.[7]

One student of the Indian warfare of this period described Quanah's tactics against the white soldier as that of "hovering around the cavalry columns, threatening . . . now and again attacking suddenly." He continued, "On one occasion, Quanah even put an arrow into Mackenzie." Quartered in the break country, he proved himself a "wily antagonist" who would attack and "then dissolve and vanish."[8]

In April of 1869, Quanah was involved in a raid into Parker County, which had been named for his own white ancestors. A pitched battle followed near Mineral Wells in which the Texan pursuers gave up the chase after the Indians turned and stood their ground. Sam Newberry, one of the Anglos, later boasted that he got one shot at Quanah.[9] That, in itself, was quite an accomplishment during the days when the son of Cynthia Ann had become an elusive legend.

By 1871, the United States government had initiated determined efforts to bring the remaining Comanches under its control. Mackenzie was instructed to see that sufficient force was used to accomplish this goal. Continued forays by the military took the trooper deeper and deeper into the land which the Indian had long considered safe territory.

J. Evetts Haley reported some of the details of Mackenzie's efforts to control Quanah's Comanche remnant during this period. The Indians proved to be adept at stealing the troopers' horses. This tactic brought considerable embarrassment to the United States Cavalry. On more than one occasion, the proud horse soldiers of the plains were forced to walk back to their fort, forgetting their dignity and becoming infantry.[10] It was during this time the Quohadi headquartered in the rugged country on the eastern side of the Llano Estacado, the Blanco Canyon area.[11]

A nearby mesa, known locally as "Soldier's Mound," was a place where Mackenzie's troops frequently found refuge from the wiles of the Quohadi. This elevation is a unique formation with a relatively flat top which would be convenient for the encampment of a sizable military force. The sides of this prominence rise sharply 150 feet or more above the surrounding prairie with only a narrow access to the mesa from the north which could be easily defended. This elevation provided protection from any enemy who would attempt to scale the slopes for a surprise attack.[12] Situated halfway between the present towns of Spur and Dickens in Dickens County, Texas, local tradition has given the mesa its name because of its military use during the final days of the Forty Year War.

During the first half of the decade of the 1870s, Quanah and his renegade band were able to successfully elude the vastly superior forces of the United States Army. When the horse soldiers did corner the Quohadi in their own environs, however, those in Quanah's Comanche remnant were able to give a good account of themselves.

In a battle which took place in the rugged, broken lands of the Blanco on October 10, 1871, Quanah captured the horse ridden by Mackenzie. Capt. R. G. Carter of the Fourth U.S. Cavalry later recalled this conflict in which Quanah shot one of his men out of the saddle and then used his body as a shield. "Otherwise," Carter declared, "I could have killed Parker as I was 30 or 40 yards from him."[13]

Later, when the Comanche chief was forced to accept life on the reservation, he offered to return the horse he had captured to General Mackenzie, who was then the post commander of Fort Sill.

Mackenzie had come to admire his former opponent, and so refused to accept the return of the mount he had lost in combat. In the final years of Quohadi independence, Quanah proudly rode the captured horse which he had named "Running Deer."[14]

In 1872, Francis A. Walker, commissioner of Indian affairs, in his official report, indicated the complexities of his problems in dealing with natives on the frontier. "There is a residue whose disposition and behavior certainly give little encouragement to further forbearance," he declared. He singled out the "Quahada Comanches, and their confederates of the Staked Plains" as the more serious sources of difficulty for the United States government as troopers sought to bring these last defiant Indians to the reservation.[15]

Mackenzie and his cavalrymen continued their attacks upon the Quohadi in an unrelenting warfare that included the burning of Indian lodges and the killing of animals whenever possible.[16]

It was to take more than military force, however, to bring the Comanche to bay. The buffalo hunter's gun was an even more effective weapon than the trooper's carbine, for, as the buffalo herds began to decrease before the onslaught of the increasing horde of frontiersmen, the ability of the Indian to exist on the South Plains became more and more precarious. Apparently, the embattled Comanche remnant was well aware of this fact.

In 1874 Quanah took a leadership role in the last of the military contests between South Plains Indians and whites. A well-organized band of Indians, which included Quohadi, attacked a heavily armed group of buffalo hunters who were fortified in abandoned buildings at Adobe Walls, on the Canadian River in the Texas panhandle.[17]

Quanah's own description of the battle, which he later reported to Capt. Hugh Scott of Fort Sill, included the following words: "We started out about 11 a.m. Stop about 4 p.m. We put saddles and blankets in trees . . . make medicine, paint faces . . . we charge down . . . that pretty hard fight."[18]

Although Quanah and his fellow warriors then had carbines, and joined a confederation of other tribes that included Kiowas, Cheyennes and Arapahos, their single-shot weapons were no match for the more advanced rifles possessed by the defenders. After a series of unsuccessful charges, the Indian combatants withdrew.[19]

The initial instigation of this battle centered around Isatai, the apostle of the Ghost Dance religion. However, his leadership was rejected when his promise of immunity from white bullets proved false. One writer, a descendant of Quanah, declared that "Quanah told the Indians Isatai was telling falsehoods . . . he then led a bunch himself" in what was apparently a final effort to dislodge the buffalo hunters.[20]

As Quanah himself put it, "Then I take all young men, go warpath to Texas."[21]

The buffalo hunter, not the cavalryman, had won the Indian war. Even the defiant Quohadi knew they could no longer exist upon the arid prairies as the great herds of buffalo began to vanish into the smoke of the hunters' guns.

On December 23, 1874, Lt. Col. J. W. Davidson penned a statement as an officer of the Tenth Cavalry that "according to reports from his men . . . the Quahadas . . . will gladly come in."[22]

Realizing the power of his white ancestors, Quanah Parker was influential in leading the Comanche remnant to reservation. Although he may not have been fully acknowledged by this time as a war chief, by using his influence to bring his people to accept pacification he became a peace chief. Two types of chiefs were recognized among Comanche tribes: war chiefs, who were courageous leaders in battle, and peace chiefs, who were effective leaders with whom the principal chief would consult in making important decisions.[23] In many ways, Quanah played both the role of war chief and peace chief.

The Quohadi remnant accepted land near Fort Sill and began the difficult task of adapting to the ways of their white conquerors. It was during these complex years of adaptation that Quanah showed evidence of true statesmanship. He was able to keep the respect of the majority of the Indians on reservation, becoming a spokesman for their causes and a defender of their rights. At the same time he was accepted as a respected leader by Anglo authorities. He was able to maintain satisfactory relations with all fourteen of the Indian agents who were responsible for the reservation during the years between 1878 and 1911. In spite of his association with governmental representatives, he continued to enjoy more popularity among his fellow tribesmen than any of the other Indian leaders, who, at least on occasion, sought to challenge his authority.[24]

Because of his statesmanlike ability to negotiate with both sides in the complexity of Indian-white relationships, he was given the title of "principal chief," the highest possible rank in Comanche culture. One student of the life of Quanah concluded that "he undoubtedly would have become a prominent band chief" had the Quohadi continued under the ancient system of independent leadership. He "would have been a leader and governor in any circle where fate might have cast him — it [was] in his blood."[25]

He traveled widely during his years as a reservation chief: he made several trips to Washington and on one occasion protested the unjust system of allotting land to the Indians in a personal visit with President McKinley.[26]

During a trip to Washington in 1890, Quanah lobbied for a revised system of land leases which resulted in the approval of his requests by the secretary of the interior. This piece of legislative manipulation initiated procedures in 1891, which made the Comanche reservation dweller's situation far more tolerable than it had been at first.[27]

He visited New Orleans, attended the Chicago World's Fair, made trips to various cities in Texas and Oklahoma, and became a friend of President Teddy Roosevelt.[28]

On one such trip, while staying in a hotel in Fort Worth with a fellow Comanche, Yellow Bear, he narrowly escaped death when his companion blew out the gas light thinking it worked like a candle. The gas, which filled the room while they slept, took the life of Yellow Bear; Quanah was resuscitated the following morning and survived the incident.[29]

The reservation chief possessed a magnificent physique, which probably accounted for his ability to survive this accident. Charles Sommer, who knew him personally, described him as "over six feet tall" and declared that he was endowed with both superior physical and mental ability.[30]

His position brought him fame and power. He built a large, twelve-room home with wide verandas two miles north of the present town of Cache, Oklahoma. He had it modeled after the residence of the commanding general of Fort Sill, Mackenzie, his old opponent. Since he insisted his followers outnumbered the soldiers at the post, he had four large stars painted on the roof of his impressive residence, making it clear he outranked the general. Because of this fact, his home became known as "The Star House."[31]

There he lived with his seven wives,[32] insisting on maintaining the Quohadi tradition of polygamy in spite of efforts by the United States government to force him to put away all but one of the women to whom he was married.

On one occasion, officials representing the United States Indian commissioner met with Quanah and strongly urged him to banish all but one of his wives. The reservation chief responded by asking how it would be possible for him to do such a thing. The Indian Department officers answered with what appeared to be a simple solution: pick out the one you love best and tell the rest that they will have to go in order to set a proper example for your people.

Quanah's reply is indicative of the character and the nature of the son of Cynthia Ann. Albert Gilles reported that the following words were a part of the chief's response:

> I have had a number of wives . . . once I had seven wives, but now I have only five . . . I love all my wives equally. I could not call my wives together and tell them, "Now that the white man is coming, his law says that I can keep but one wife. White man says I should keep the one that I love best. The rest are surplus and must go and live somewhere else. So this is the woman I love the best, and the rest of you are surplus. You must go and live elsewhere." This I can not do. You come to my house. You pick out a wife for me to keep. Then you tell 'em.[33]

In 1890 Commissioner Thomas J. Morgan ordered Quanah fired as principal chief of the Comanches because of his refusal to

give up the practice of polygamy. Agent Charles E. Adams, however, protested: "Any other Comanche would also be ineligible."
Adams' logic finally won out and Quanah was restored to his position of leadership, allowing him to keep his house full of wives.[34]

He remained as principal chief throughout his life. After his
death, Superintendent Ernest Stecker proposed that the government not recognize another chief. With the adoption of this recom-
mendation, Quanah became the last chief of the Comanches.[35]

Charles Goodnight recalled that Quanah was noted for being
gentle with women. He "never allowed any women to be killed . . .
I personally know of two that he had two or three days in the woods
and turned loose, showing them the way home."[36] A Mrs. Dan
Coke, who once visited Quanah in his home, later recalled that he
was polite and gracious.[37]

His interest in women was legendary, and, on one occasion,
this quality created an international problem. One young woman,
Too-ni-ce, who was married to an Indian man who reportedly mis-
treated her, went to Quanah's house before daylight and tapped on
the window in order to seek his protection. He took her from the
area, purchased expensive clothing for her, and went with her to
Mexico for an extended sojourn. This caused concern for both the
United States Indian Department and officials of the Mexican government. An extensive search began for the runaway chief and his
female associate. Eventually, through the cooperation of both gov-
ernments, the couple was located and both were returned to the
reservation. Quanah finally made Too-ni-ce a legal wife, and, according to a contemporary who later recalled this incident, she
"reigned supreme in his home until his death."[38]

All of the descriptions of Quanah indicate that he was hand-
some and well proportioned. One account declared that he "was
the finest looking man in all the Comanche tribe; tall, straight,
darker than many warriors and with dignity in his features . . ."[39]

One of the roads leading to the southwest corner of the old
quadrangle of Fort Sill has been named Quanah Road. According
to a statement recorded in the post archives, it was along this route
that the Comanche chief and his wives would travel from their

home in Cache to visit the post commander. The army gave him a "Dougherty wagon which resembled a stagecoach . . . hitched behind a four horse team [in which he] and his wives rode in state on ceremonial occasions."[40]

Quanah was able to bridge the gap between the traditional culture of the Comanche and the demands placed upon him by his conquerors. He continued to maintain his Indian identity while learning the complexities of life on the reservation, which included the legal aspects of land leases and right-of-ways.[41]

He was deeply interested in anything he considered to be of value to his people. He played an important role in developing a pan-Indian religion which had among its rituals the cultic use of peyote.[42] Quanah imported the drug from Mexico through a merchant in Laredo, Texas, who wrote him in February 1907, "regretting that Peyotes which were sent out were spoiled" and promising "to replace with good ones."[43]

J. J. Methwin described the use of the drug in a ritual at which Quanah was present. Worshipers entered a tepee to the noise of the tom-tom and sat in a circle with eyes closed. There were songs and an explanation of the "inspiration from the Great Father." A large peyote button was then placed on a horseshoe furnace. After worship the women had an ample supply of food, a portion of which was "offered to the sun." When all was over, those who had participated found it necessary to lie down to "sleep off the effects of the drug."[44]

On one occasion Quanah defended the experiential element in Indian religion with these words: "The white man goes into his church house and talks about Jesus, but the Indian goes into his tepee and talks to Jesus."[45]

The Comanche chief was responsible for chartering the Native American Church, which was an effort to develop religious concerns among Indians of various tribes by drawing upon the spiritual heritage of their primitive faith. The use of the peyote ritual, which was a part of such a heritage, was one of the factors which made this development highly suspect by other religious groups.[46]

This denominational organization still continues late in the twentieth century as the Native American Church of North America and is the only group entitled to use peyote in religious ritual under United States law. Only certified members of the church, which consists of some 300,000 Indians in thirty-five tribes, are allowed to purchase the drug from legally licensed dealers who secure it from growers in South Texas between Laredo and Rio Grande City. In the 1980s an Arizona-based group filed suit seeking to secure the same privilege which had been granted to the church founded by Quanah for the use of the drug, but observers of the effort to legalize peyote on a wider scale believe federal law will remain firm on this issue.[47]

Quanah made every effort to secure information concerning his mother during his reservation years. Through the help of his father's former antagonist, Sul Ross, he secured a photograph of Cynthia Ann and his sister, Topsannah, made by a photographer soon after their capture.[48]

In June of 1908, Quanah received the information he had been seeking concerning the death and burial of Cynthia Ann. J. R. O'Quinn wrote the Comanche chief from Rio Vista, Texas, stating that "she was living with my father and mother when she died." He then assured Quanah, as a response to the chief's advertisement for information about the burial location, "we can site you to the place."[49]

A. C. Birdsong, a Parker relative, aided Quanah in both the location of the grave and the removal of the body. He reported to the chief that he had precise information about the site since there were the "carved letters C. A. P. on a flat rock [which had been] placed over the grave."[50]

At some time during the year 1909, the bones of Cynthia Ann were exhumed and transported to the reburial site near Cache, Oklahoma, under the supervision of Birdsong assisted by Knox Beal, a resident of Cache.[51] On February 10, 1909, the Texas legislature appropriated $1,000 to build a grave monument memorializing the life of Cynthia Ann.[52]

A. C. Birdsong personally supervised the opening of the grave. He later declared in a notarized statement, "I found proof that the remains of Prairie Flower [Topsannah] were in a grave beside hers [Cynthia Ann's]. I had no authority [to do so], but I decided to put the remains of the mother and daughter together and have them shipped to Cache, Oklahoma."[53]

When the remains were shown to Quanah by Birdsong, the Comanche chief asked if he could be sure about an identification. When he received an affirmative answer, Quanah said simply: "Then I am satisfied. I have looked for her for a long time."[54]

The body of Cynthia Ann, intermingled with the bones of Topsannah, was buried at the direction of the last of the Comanche chiefs a short distance west of the Star House.[55] On the occasion of his mother's reburial, Quanah was quoted as declaring: "Comanche may die today, tomorrow, ten years. When end comes, then they all be together again. I want to see my mother again then."[56]

On January 7, 1911, Quanah wrote to his friend Charles Goodnight declaring, "I have already moved my mother's remains to Oklahoma. I am going to put a high marble monument on my mother's grave." He then added in the same letter, "I am getting old and I am not able to do anything much."[57]

Quanah died soon after he had penned the letter to Goodnight.[58] His death certificate carried the date February 23, 1911.[59]

When the fact of his death was known, expressions of regret came to his survivors from across the land. The House of Representatives of the State of Oklahoma went on record during its Thirty-second Session in 1911 declaring "regret at the death of the Great Chief."[60]

Quanah was buried beside the relocated grave of his mother. When the United States government took over the land upon which he had lived, the graves of the Comanche leader and those of his mother and sister were moved to the Chief's Knoll in the Post Cemetery at Fort Sill.[61]

A confidential army memo was penned at the time, addressed to the "Engineers exhuming the remains of Quanah Parker and his mother," saying that "it is possible an effort might be made to steal the remains and hide them for reburial secretly . . . I suggest the graves be under guard."[62] This precaution was probably based on the fact Quanah's grave had been desecrated four years after his death. However, immediately after that act, his descendants secured a new casket and carefully and solemnly reburied their last chief.[63]

Three memorial stones are clearly visible upon entering the Chief's Knoll area of the Post Cemetery at Fort Sill. On the largest of the stones, an impressive granite monument[64] erected above the burial place of Quanah, these words are engraved: "Resting here until the day breaks and shadows fall and darkness disappears is QUANAH PARKER, Last Chief of the Comanches."

Next to this monument, there are two smaller ones. Inscriptions upon them read: "Cynthia Ann Parker" and "Toh-Tsee-ah."[65]

Clearly, the three are now reunited in peaceful repose.

The son had found his mother. He had brought her to his home to rest among his people.

And his people, the Comanches, were her people.

XIV.

A Separate Ember

The grasslands of the Oklahoma prairie still stretch westward from Fort Sill. A land with few trees and only occasional irregularities, it has about it the quality of a sunlit sea as it continues toward the horizon where it blends into the sky as though the two were destined to be one. In the distance, the gentle slopes of the Wichitas stand brooding over the land as though these hills shared the tragedy of the vanquished Comanche nation.

It was there that the remnant of the once proud Indians of the South Plains were forced to live. Their adjustment to the requirements of their Anglo captors was slow and difficult. Many died in the process. Those who did not succumb to the diseases of the white man were only able to survive with great difficulty: this they did simply by exercising the innate ingenuity which is characteristic of the peoples of the prairies.

Quanah's Star House was more than a good-natured questioning of a general's military authority: it was a declaration that the Indian would live upon the reservation with at least some degree of dignity. For a brief time it became the focal point of survival in the restricted environment in which the conquered remnant found themselves.

It was on land west of the Star House, in the same plot where Cynthia Ann was reburied, that the body of the son was laid to rest only months after he had superintended the placing of her remains in the grave. His bones would lie near the intermingled bones of his mother and sister until removal to the Chief's Knoll at Fort Sill.

Although the Anglo descendants of the frontiersmen who had usurped the prairies readily agreed to the symbolic act of transporting Cynthia Ann's body to Indian territory, this was no compensation for that which had happened.

For the mother of Quanah, this was a reunion which was half a century too late.

During her final years before death, she became an increasingly tragic figure. Although her natal family made every effort to reclaim her for white society, this was a transition which, for her, was impossible.

Her Anglo contemporaries had found it difficult to understand why she had refused to return to her natal culture when she had opportunity to do so. For them it was beyond reason for anyone who had been raised in the relative comfort of white civilization to deliberately choose to remain a member of a nomadic tribe living in one of the more barren areas of the continent.

Even more amazing to some was the fact that Cynthia Ann sought to return to the prairie after her recapture. Perhaps her immediate family understood, for they were of pioneering stock. Their parents had risked all to come to the frontier. But, for most of her Anglo contemporaries, there was no comprehension of why she was determined to reject the society to which she had been forcibly returned.

Perhaps in every age there are those who cannot understand why comfort and ease should not be among the primary goals of life. Such thinking still dominates late twentieth-century culture which continues to measure ultimate worth in terms of material possessions and physical security.

Is it conceivable that anyone in any age would prefer a primitive, nomadic life away from the comforts of a more highly developed material existence?

Cynthia Ann cannot be explained merely in terms of her admiration for a simple lifestyle among a unique people. This, in itself, is not enough.

The record of this saga presents yet another factor. This was the fact that Cynthia Ann not only found a home among the nomadics of the Plains, but she became one of them.

She became an Indian.

This was a conscious choice. As a young woman she had known both lifestyles. By accepting her place among the Quohadi, she deliberately rejected one and chose the other.

This was more than a stoic acceptance of Comanche culture, a willingness to do whatever was necessary to exist, a determination to survive at all costs.

The prairie sun not only changed the tint of her skin but penetrated into her very being, giving her the ability to become a Comanche both physically and spiritually. Because of this fact, when the last link to the life she had once lived was broken, she sorrowed even unto death.

In her final months she continued to think and act as an Indian. This was her ultimate rejection of the social structure to which she had been forcibly returned.

She found solace only in her lonely vigil beside the grave of Topsannah.

Her last days were visionary ones. It was then she felt once more the wind of the sunlit plains, sensed again the vastness of the shadowless prairie, recalled the magnificence of a cloudless sky.

She remembered campfires upon the prairie where the warmth of the fire dispelled the chill of the night. But she knew that when a log rolled away from the flame, it quickly became an ember which would soon lose its glow. It became dark and faded into the shades of the night.

In her final months she believed herself to be an ember separate, one apart from the flame.

Even in her aloneness, she found within the depths of her

being the ability to seek a vision. In keeping with Comanche custom, she went frequently to her solitary place of meditation. There she found solace for her grieving soul in the isolation she imposed upon herself near the grave of Topsannah.

There she sought, and doubtless found, her vision.

Could it have been a vision of what she hoped for her first-born, Quanah, the one who had remained on the prairie with his father even after the guns of the white militia had ceased to belch their smoke?

Could there have been a mystical glimpse of a time yet to come when there would be a great last chief of the Comanches, one who would lead his people toward peace?

If such an experience had come to the one who believed herself to be an ember apart from the flame, could it not have included a dream that she would yet be reunited with her own in the warmth of the land, even when there was no sunshine on the prairie?

If such was her vision, it was one which was fulfilled.

When her bones, intermingled with those of her youngest off-spring, were transported for reburial to the land of the Comanche at the request of Quanah, her dream was consummated.

Her son had long sought her.

Although it was half a century too late, it was a reunion.

The wind still comes fresh across the grasslands which stretch westward from the military post.

The prairie reaches beyond the gentle contours of the Wichitas which yet brood over the trail's end.

There is peace upon the land.

XV.

End of an Era

For the embattled Quohadi remnant, the trail ended at the gates of Fort Sill. When Quanah and those who had challenged Mackenzie and his troopers in the arroyos of Blanco Canyon surrendered, the independence which their ancestors had known for centuries upon the South Plains was no more.

In referring to the events of 1874–1875 which brought the remnant of the Comanches to the reservation, a direct descendant of the union of Cynthia Ann and Nocona made this declaration: "That was the end of an era of a beautiful life they once lived."[1]

It would not be the only expression of regret over the demise of the culture of the natives of the South Plains. There were many others.

Even among the enemies of the Indian, there were those who had become enamored with the society which they had been commissioned to destroy.

Robert Goldthwaite Carter, a member of the military forces assigned the task of bringing the last of the Comanches to reservation, wrote ecstatically of "the nomadic redman [who] lived his free and careless life" upon the South Plains.[2] Elsewhere in his printed work, he referred in highly nostalgic terms to the existence of the "nomadic Quo-ha-da" who ranged through the Blanco Canyon area of Texas.[3]

G. A. Holland, in an account of the war between settler and Indian, spoke in similar terms of the Quohadi as a people who enjoyed unrestricted freedom.[4] Indian fighters such as Sul Ross, Kit Carson, and John Ford, who had risked their lives to conquer the Comanche, developed a high degree of admiration for the courage and the tenacity of those they sought to destroy.

This was more than an appreciation of the bravery of the Indian. Often there was a note of regret in their statements which verged on apologies for having had a part in the final destruction of the freedom of these people.

Certainly, the Quohadi were a uniquely self-sufficient and independent people. But their self-sufficiency was more than the physical quality of their nomadicism, for there was about them a singular spirituality which was a part of their psyche.

It was this self-determinate freedom of spirit which made it possible for people such as the Quohadi to continue to exist in the rugged lands of Blanco Canyon, the breaks of the South Plains, and the arid fringes of the Llano Estacado until the last quarter of the nineteenth century.

It was this quality which enthralled Cynthia Ann and led her to become an integral part of the very society which had made her a captive.

The strategy of the destruction of the buffalo herds along with the overwhelming firepower of the United States military brought a final end both to their identity as a people and their independence.

XVI.

The Ghosts of Blanco Canyon

They say there are ghosts in the canyon.

In recent years there are those who claim to have seen the figure of a mounted Indian on one of the many promontories within the broken lands of Blanco Canyon.

It is through this canyon that the White River runs on its way to becoming the Salt Fork of the Brazos River.

This is a part of the break country of West Texas, an irregular area which marks the southern and eastern extremities of the South Plains.

Erosion of both wind and water have created draws and arroyos which continually challenge the eminence of the Caprock which overlooks the area. The high plains stretch in endless evenness for hundreds of miles beyond the Caprock. Further to the south and east there are the gently rolling farm lands which make up much of Central Texas. The break country is neither. Nor is it in any way akin to the fertile country of North and East Texas, which, in recent years, has become heavily populated.

In the breaks, one can see an occasional flat-topped mesa

standing in lonely isolation which appears to have wandered away from the Llano Estacado.

It is a land of mesquite and cacti, of outcroppings of sandstone and shale. Occasionally these give way to water holes and small streams which only become effusive after thunderstorms on the high prairie have sent torrents of water into the area.

The break country is a land that still is sparsely populated. It is an area of stock farms and ranches which have proven to be profitable only where oil has been discovered. During most of the nineteenth century, this was a land almost unknown to white settlers.

Although the depressions in the break country are less pronounced than the dramatic formations of the famed Palo Duro Canyon that bisects a portion of the South Plains in the Texas panhandle, this land, nevertheless, has its places of rocky protrusion.

One of these is the Blanco, a site of lonely ruggedness only a few miles west of the present town of Dickens. South of Dickens there is a somewhat larger community, Spur, named for a cattle ranch which operated in the area around the turn of the century. Between the two towns there is the mesa known as Soldier's Mound, which, because of its sentinel-like isolation, can be seen from miles around. It was there that Mackenzie's troops camped when they sought to conquer the Quohadi.[1]

From the town of Dickens, one can take the road west which runs along a track that rises quickly to the top of the Caprock. For a few miles there is nothing but the flatness of the unending prairie, until suddenly there is a great expanse of broken land bounded by sharp outcroppings of sandstone and rusty soil.

This is Blanco Canyon. It is here that local legend claims the ghosts of the past still linger.

White River is no more than a cautious stream as it flows through the center of the canyon, forming an oasis with its regular supply of fresh water. There one can always find green grass which lends vivid contrast to an area surrounded by arid and forbidding lands.

The legends claim that, on occasion, one can see the form of an Indian which may suddenly appear on some irregular prominence, or may be glimpsed beside a bend in the small stream. There are those in the area who claim they can discern from time to time the figure of a rider on horseback. On occasion, they may sight a lonely sentinel peering through the shadows in the direction of distant Soldier's Mound from which cavalrymen might suddenly appear. Or, possibly, when there is no more than a thin sliver of a moon, one might see an encampment of irregular tepees appearing in the mists of late evening with lazy spirals of smoke rising above them.

One has but to visit the Blanco Canyon area of the break country and linger for a time, perhaps as a pale, misty moon breaks through the occasional clouds to balance the glory of the light newly faded in the western sky, to be convinced of the reality of these apparitions.

One cannot be sure, for the visions that come in the light of a frail moon may soon fade away. Always, with the coming of the full light of the sun, they are gone. But then, if these be the spirits of nomads, nomads have always managed to disappear when the harshness of noon comes upon the land.

If the visions have any substance, certainly they are those of the proud and courageous Quohadi.

There is no doubt that Quanah's last remnant of Comanches spent some time in Blanco Canyon.[2] There is evidence that this was their final place of encampment after the Anglo military had discovered Palo Duro, Peace River, Antelope Hill, and other places of Comanche refuge. From headquarters in this area, the last efforts of an embattled people were made to reclaim their land and to maintain their existence.

It is little wonder that twentieth-century inhabitants of the break country have sensed the spirits of those who once dwelt there.[3] Quanah's father, Nocona, and his band of Quohadi likely had camped there on occasion before the son's final efforts to stave off the advance of the white hunter drove him and his remnant to the Blanco. Almost certainly, Cynthia Ann and the others who were a part of that nomadic group of Indians who survived long beyond their time, watered there, found repose on the grass of the canyon's uneven floor, saw the glory of sunsets from the canyon's recesses, and sensed the mystic magnificence of the Blanco.

Who can say that they are no more?

Who would dare claim that the spirits of the Indian past have ceased to exist?

Who could honestly believe that the unbelievable courage and dauntless spirit possessed by these people has actually passed from this earth?

If you think such is possible, go west of Dickens. Find an evening when the sun has sunk below the horizon amidst the glory of the West Texas sky.

Wait patiently until the moon casts its eerie beams across the prairie beyond the canyon rim.

If you would dare do such a thing, you will not for a moment declare that Nocona, Quanah — the people Cynthia Ann made her own — are no more. Certainly, their spirits live.

Perhaps the true enigma of Cynthia Ann is not so much a question of why a nine-year-old white girl completely adopted the ways of the Quohadi and then refused to leave those she considered to be her own to return to her natal relatives.

Nor is it a question of why Cynthia Ann preferred a nomadic life on the plains over a sedimentary existence in white civilization.

Perhaps the real mystery is why others did not do the same.

More specifically, why is it we have allowed the spirit of Nocona, which enthralled Cynthia Ann, to die? Or have such spirits died?

Perhaps the ghosts are more than figments of imagination. Possibly, just possibly, the spirit of the Quohadi, the dauntless courage that was theirs, the unbelievable will to survive against all odds, still exists.

Do not doubt it unless you have dared to seek the ghosts of Blanco Canyon.

Afterword

The author's daughter, Annetta, shortly after graduation from Southern Methodist University, was discussing future plans with a classmate, Randy. A copy of a book about Cynthia Ann Parker lay on a nearby coffee table in the family parlor where the two sat.

Randy noticed the volume and mentioned the fact he was related to the Parkers. Annetta replied she shared a similar heritage.

Randy could remember a grandfather who was the son of Quanah Parker and was able to relate accounts of his ancestors who had descended from the union of Cynthia Ann and Peta Nocona.

Annetta was a direct descendant of Silas Bates, one of the pioneers who came with the Parkers to Texas. He had been present at the time of the raid on the fort by renegade Comanches in 1836. It was Silas Bates who had helped save other members of Cynthia Ann's family from capture. According to family tradition, he later married the youngest of the Parker daughters he had helped save. The Bates ancestry represented the Anglo side of the early Texas saga.

In May 1979, Annetta and Randy married.

Perhaps in some mystic way two great strains in the history of the Southwest have now become one.

Appendix I

The Death of Nocona

What were the circumstances surrounding the death of Peta Nocona?

At no point in the story of Cynthia Ann is there a greater divergence between the Anglo record and the Indian account than in the reporting of the demise of the Quohadi chief.

Sul Ross and his ranger company, who attacked the Quohadi encampment on the Pease River in 1860, believed they had killed the wily chieftain during the raid.

James T. DeShields, in a book published in 1886, declared that Nocona died during the encounter, and gave some very convincing details of the death scene which reportedly came from eyewitnesses. According to this work, written while most of the principals were still living, Nocona was shot from his mount during the brief encounter. He then shot arrows toward the white raiders until he was too badly wounded to continue to fight. Pulling himself upright against a tree, he continued his defiance by refusing to surrender. A blast of buckshot ended his life.[1]

DeShields listed in his work an impressive array of contemporaries as sources for his account that included Ross himself, John Ford, and Walter Lane.

It is worth noting that DeShields lived long enough to see a reprinting of his work in 1934, a half century after he had penned his original account. He sanctioned this republication, and in so doing, reaffirmed his conviction that his account was accurate.

In 1931 a report of Nocona's death was published in which Felix Williams and Hervey Chesley recorded a firsthand account of the Pease River battle based on information from Benjamin Franklin Gholson. His recollections were in substantial agreement with DeShields. Apparently, Gholson was aware of other accounts of the conflict, and after telling his story, he declared emphatically: "That is the way them boys and Sull [sic] told it!"[2]

Other writers accepted this version of Nocona's death without question.

However, after Quanah Parker had been influential in leading the last of the Comanches to reservation, he insisted that his father had not died in the Pease River battle.

Baldwin Parker, son of Quanah, writing from Cache, Oklahoma, to Rupert Richardson, December 20, 1941, cited a statement made by his father on July 9, 1986, in which he declared that Nocona had survived the Pease River raid.[3]

Quanah made this declaration on several occasions, insisting that his father had not been killed in 1860.

The Gholson account admitted that none of the rangers present had seen or known Nocona, and that there was no serious effort to make a positive identification of the body. In addition, the circumstances of the conflict would lend considerable doubt to the conviction of Sul Ross that he had participated in the death of the Quohadi war chief: the brief battle was fought during a violent sandstorm and the white raiders did not linger for long at the site of the decimated Comanche encampment.[4]

No less an authority than Charles Goodnight has been credited with making the following statement: "Nocona . . . was not even at the Pease River fight, as he had left the party two days before with his two boys, Quanah and Peanut."[5]

In 1926 Goodnight dictated a statement to J. Evetts Haley relating to the Pease River encounter: "Nocona . . . was not there at the time . . . but had left two days before with his two boys . . . he lived many years afterwards and died while out on a plum hunt."[6]

In another statement, Goodnight, who gained his information from Quanah, declared that the aging chieftain, on one occasion, stated he saw his father die "two or three years" after the Pease River battle and that "he was buried near the Antelope Hills."[7]

Rupert Richardson, writing about the death of Nocona in an article in the *Southwestern Historical Quarterly*, concluded that "the Indian . . . killed was not Chief Nocona. Quanah . . . was 12 years old at the time . . . [and he] certainly knew what he was talking about, [when he] stated repeatedly in later years that his father Nocona, was not killed in the attack and that he lived for several years after it."[8]

Although Ross and his men believed they had killed the Quohadi chief, and probably convinced others of their exploit, Peta Nocona lived for at least two or three years after the raid.[9] During this time he sought to avenge the attack on his people. He continued to be an elusive figure of Indian power as troops were withdrawn from the West Texas area to fight America's Civil War.

There seems to be little doubt that he was not present at the time of the Ross attack on the Quohadi encampment in 1860, and that the defender killed by the rangers was not Nocona.

Appendix II

The Birth of Quanah

There is a wide divergence of information relating to the birth of Quanah Parker. Dates have been cited for his birth that range all of the way from the mid-1840s to the year 1856.

Charles Sommer, who knew the Comanche chief personally, and who asserted that he gained information for his printed work from Quanah himself, stated his birth date was 1852,[1] and that the reservation chief died at the age of sixty in 1911.[2] The Quanah monument above his grave in Fort Sill was engraved with this date.

Some writers, however, have given even later dates, one setting his birth year as 1856.[3]

The plaque on the Star House in which Quanah died, now located in Cache, Oklahoma, gives the date 1850 for the year of his birth. This marker was probably based on Quanah's belief that he was "born about 1850," a statement which he made to Charles Goodnight.[4] However, this was only an estimate, for Quanah himself was not at all certain about the exact year of his birth.

Since Cynthia Ann was captured in 1836 and reached maturity either in 1840 or 1841, the time at which she would have been given to Nocona for marriage, a date even earlier than 1845 would be possible. All other data points to a birth date for Quanah in the mid-1840s. Ruling out the possibility of multiple miscarriages (of which there is no evidence) and considering the fact that Quanah was considered the oldest offspring of the union of Nocona and Cynthia Ann, it is highly unlikely that Quanah could have been born any later than 1846. His obituary in the Lawton (Oklahoma) *News* dated February 28, 1911, gave his age at the time of his death as sixty-seven and stated that he was fourteen years of age at the time his mother was captured by rangers in 1860.[5] This would place the date of his birth as either late in the year 1844 or early in 1845. This time frame would fit other evidence relating to his life and the information available concerning his mother.

Because of the nomadic movement of the Quohadi upon the plains, there is no definitive information concerning the site of Quanah's birth. One tradition preserved in the Olive King Dixon Papers declared that the Comanche chief was born at "Cache Creek in Indian Territory."[6] This statement was based on information from Charles Goodnight, who reportedly quoted Quanah as having commented that "from the best information I have, I was born . . . on Elk Creek just below the Wichita Mountains."[7]

Quanah's own uncertainty about his birth site would raise a question about the accuracy of the Dixon tradition.

The Wichita Mountains were at the eastern extremity of Comanche territory in the 1840s. The Quohadi seldom ranged that far to the east, preferring to remain on the high plains south of the Canadian River and centering their movements around the Palo Duro.[8] A United States commission described the "Comanche Range" as "southward from the Canadian River through the South Plains and into Central Texas."[9]

Another tradition describing the birth site of the chieftain has been preserved in a manuscript letter in the Quanah Papers in the archives of Fort Sill, Oklahoma. This document states that his birth took place at "Cedar Lake or Laguna Sabinas," a small high plains watering spot located twenty miles south of the site of the present town of Brownfield, Texas.[10] This information would coincide with the data that is available regarding the Quohadi range at the time Cynthia Ann reached maturity.

The last chief of the Comanches was probably born at Cedar Lake or at a site in that general geographical area, either late in the year 1844 or before the end of 1845.

Appendix III

The Literature of White Captives

A considerable body of materials relate the experiences of white captives taken by Indians during the middle years of the nineteenth century. Among these are several accounts which give information about the treatment Cynthia Ann would have received and the kind of life she would have lived during her years on the South Plains.

Immediately after Rachel Plummer published her *Narrative* in 1838, a writer by the name of E. House authored a work which described the experiences of two white women, a Mrs. Horn and a Mrs. Harris, as captives among the Comanches.[1]

Soon afterward, T. A. Babb, a young Anglo, wrote about his experiences in a work entitled *In the Bosom of the Comanches*.[2] A later publication of a similar nature was entitled *Lost and Found, or Three Months with the Wild Indians*. This work was written by a Texan named Ole T. Nystel, who was only slightly older than Cynthia Ann at the time of his capture. A second edition of Nystel's work, under the title *From Bondage to Freedom or Three Months with Wild Indians,* was published soon after the first, indicating the popularity of his writings.[3]

Nystel's experiences paralleled those of the young Parker girl, at least in the early stage of her existence among the Plains Indians. His writings give a unique insight into the life she would have lived on the prairie. He was captured by raiding Comanches in a violent attack on a white settlement. Although others were killed in the raid, he survived. He then was forced to travel a great distance to a camp on the South Plains.[4]

The writings which relate the misfortunes of female hostages such as Plummer, Harris, and Horn give insight into the events which took place in the life of Cynthia Ann as a young girl and as a woman. These records offer an important look into the conditions imposed on women captives by the tribesmen of the South Plains.

A number of other mid-nineteenth-century works give additional information regarding Cynthia Ann's life as a Comanche. Among these are Ben Moore's *Seven Years with the Wild Indians,*[5] Marvin J. Hunter's *The Boy Captives*, Herman Lehmann's *Nine Years Among the Indians,* and Edwin Eastman's *Seven and Nine Years Among the Comanches and Apaches*. Hugh Corwin's work entitled *Comanche and Kiowa Captives* gives important information about the experiences of other white hostages who lived for extended periods of time among the Indians. In addition, there are extant references to the adventures of captives who lived among the Comanches, such as those of the Mooar Brothers who were near contemporaries of Cynthia Ann.[6]

Some of these accounts include tales which are of questionable reliability, since the widespread interest in white hostages during this period encouraged narrators to add a bit of color to the telling of their stories. However, in most cases these were creditable accounts and the basic facts are accurate. This body of literature adds a great deal to the knowledge of Indian-Anglo relations on the southwestern frontier and is essential to an understanding of the life of Cynthia Ann Parker.

Appendix IV

Comanche Religion and the Ghost Dance

Perhaps no more critical account of Comanche life has ever been written than that which was produced by Rachel Plummer. Her vivid descriptions of mistreatment during captivity had much to do with the determination of her white contemporaries to continue their war of extermination against the Indians who had captured her.

It is significant, however, that Plummer wrote favorably about one aspect of Comanche life: the tribal religious consciousness. In her narrative she indicated she was impressed with the spirituality of these people, who, she reported, were able to doctor "by faith," and who had a variety of primitive means of bringing about renewed health.[1]

Sanapia, a Comanche healer on the reservation during Quanah's days of leadership of the tribal remnant, left an extensive account of the ritualistic use of drugs, herbs, salves, and other religious rites related both to physical and spiritual therapeutic practices. Since the information she provided was based on generations of tribal tradition, this record gives considerable insight into Comanche religion.

Sanapia described both the rites and the procedures involved in Comanche healing. Ointments were applied with four movements of the hand since the number four was considered a mystical number. Peyote was used both ceremonially and as a remedy for pain and distress. Tea made from plant roots and remedies which were the products of various botanical species were administered for particular maladies. Sometimes Comanche doctors would use their mouths "to suck sickness from the body" of a patient.[2]

A class of healing practitioners existed in Comanche culture not unlike those of other North American tribes. These medicine men, or sometimes medicine women,[3] served both as religious and health specialists, and would advise the tribal leadership concerning ceremonial acts considered essential to the well being of the tribe.[4]

Burial practices were based on religious rites. The Plains Indians generally wrapped their dead ceremonially in several blankets and either "took them to the mountains,"[5] or placed the corpses on a scaffold some six feet above the ground, leaving their earthly possessions nearby.[6] One writer claimed that the horse of the departed was sometimes killed and the body placed with the possessions so that "these things were to meet the warrior in the happy hunting grounds."[7] It was only after the Comanche had been forced to accept life on the reservation that they were required to use cemeteries.[8]

Comanche spiritual practices, however, went far beyond physical healing and ceremonies for the burial of the dead. Rachel Plummer recognized in her hated tormentors a genuine belief in a Supreme Being.[9] Other contemporary accounts agreed with this observation. Charles Sommer, a later associate of Quanah Parker, stated that the Quohadi worshiped the "Indian God Niatpol."[10]

Wayne Parker, a direct descendant of Quanah, declared that his ancestor before a battle would "pray to the Great Spirit for guidance and a sign to show him the way." He followed the Comanche practice of seeking divine direction through natural signs: the howling of a wolf or the darting of an eagle from the sky. In making his decision to lead his people to reservation, Wayne Parker claimed, Quanah saw that a "bird flew northeast toward Fort Sill. This was a sign from the Great Spirit, and Quanah obeyed."[11]

Ole Nystel, in his record of experiences with these people, attested to deep religious convictions among the Comanches, part of which he attributed to the fact they were "superstitious and ready to relegate anything not easily accounted for to the supernatural." He was convinced that his survival was due to his ability to convince his captors that he was "under the protection of the Great Spirit."[12]

Cynthia Ann, captured at the age when formal religious thought first appears,[13] would have developed her personal religious consciousness during her period of adjustment to life as a Comanche. As a young girl, she was reared in the vigorous religious atmosphere of the Parker family, who were establishing a fundamentalist Baptist church in Texas based upon a simplistic, non-missionary theology. The trauma of her captivity would have forced the blending of these teachings with the primitive faith of the Indian in a Great Spirit. This would have given her the stamina to endure and survive her new life upon the plains. The intensity of her religious experience is supported by a tradition which was recorded in the Fort Sill papers: "Cynthia Ann tattooed a cross on her children's arms — with gunpowder or something — 'branded them' . . . [for such a symbol was discovered on Quanah] at Fort Sill when they gave him a physical exam."[14]

Although the rites of the Comanches were simple, and the religion they practiced was related to nature, there is much evidence of a deep appreciation of the spiritual.

The ceremony of the Cedar Smoke is one such ritual which has continued to this day among the Comanche descendants. In this act, a clump of closely tied cedar leaves is slowly burned until the sweet aroma of the cedar permeates whatever object or group is to be blessed.[15] Quanah himself cedar smoked the town that bears his name in a ceremony in 1884, after he had become a respected leader of a reservation tribe. His grandson, Baldwin Parker, Jr., returned to the same place to perform an identical ceremony a century later in 1984.[16]

Twentieth-century Comanches still practice the rite of Cedar Smoking, according to information available from descendants of the South Plains Indians now living in Oklahoma. A report in 1986 described how an adopted daughter of descendants of Quanah was "Cedar Smoked" as an act of her full acceptance both into the family and the tribe.[17]

After Quanah became a reservation chief, he used his influence as the principal chief of his people to perpetuate the Indian religious practices he had grown up with. He sought to bring other Native Americans into participation in a Pan-Indian religion which would continue the rites and observances of their ancestors.[18]

It was during this period that he chartered the Native American Church, which was an effort to combine the spiritual heritage of the Indian with the organizational procedures of white Americans.[19] The ritual use of peyote had traditionally been a part of this cult.

Quanah was influential in securing a repeal of anti-peyote laws which would have prohibited the ritualistic use of the drug even by the Indian. In 1908 he testified before the Oklahoma state legislature in behalf of the right of the Comanche people to continue the use of peyote in religious practices.[20] Quanah had difficulty securing the drug in Oklahoma, but was able to import peyote from Mexico through merchants in Laredo, Texas, in the early 1900s.[21]

Late in the twentieth century, the Native American Church still has the exclusive legal right to use peyote in their rituals and to continue to purchase it from the Laredo area through licensed dealers, although this privilege is being challenged by other groups in the federal courts. A series of court cases have dealt with the right of the Indian to be exempt from strictures placed on other United States citizens in regard to the regulated and ritualistic use of peyote. These have generally been decided in favor of the Native American.[22]

It is significant that the claim to leadership during the final days of Comanche life on the plains was related to spiritual power. Tribal leadership, particularly in a time of crisis, often centered around an individual who could convince his associates that he possessed a special type of spirituality. The final South Plains conflict at Adobe Walls was largely instigated by an Indian named Isatai who "announced that he possessed power to help the Indians overcome the Whites."[23]

This was a type of spiritualism which had been manifest early in the nineteenth century among the Shawnee followers of Tecumseh and which was continued into the 1880s by the practitioners of Wovoka's Ghost Dance religion. Isatai called the Comanches together and scheduled a sun dance; he then led the more warlike in smearing their bodies with mud and willow leaves, and worked them into a frenzy in preparation for battle. He, himself, went naked into battle after he had smeared both his own body and that of his horse with yellow paint. Because of his claims and his promise of glory through spiritual means, he was able to lead a sizable contingent of Comanche warriors to the final South Plains battle between Indians and whites at Adobe Walls.[24]

One authority on the Indian culture of this period declared that the Ghost Dance religion had a special appeal to the Comanches because they believed this gave promise of the hope that a messiah would "restore the buffalo with all their former customs."[25]

Clearly, the tenets of this nineteenth-century Native American spiritualism did have an impact on the South Plains Indians, at least in the third quarter of the century. Cynthia Ann's own tribe was impacted at some point by the unique claims of this militant religiosity.

By the 1870s, apostles of the Ghost Dance religion had contacted the Quohadi remnants. Whether or not Cynthia Ann was ever effected by this faith, it is clear that Quanah was in contact with Isatai, who led the attack on the white hunters in the 1874 conflict at Adobe Walls. Dee Brown's history of the west from the Indian viewpoint assumed a close relationship between Quanah and Isatai in preparing for the battle.[26] It was the Indian messiah, Isatai, who inspired the Comanche remnants to undertake this last effort to stem the tide of Anglo invasion on the plains. The son of Cynthia Ann, however, played a major role in the battle by leading a portion of the braves into the fight.[27]

The Indian spiritualism of Isatai was not sufficient to ward off the bullets of the repeating rifles of the whites. The Comanches finally withdrew in utter defeat, an event which not only discredited the Ghost Dance faith, but brought a final sense of hopelessness to the remnant of the tribe.

When the last spiritual force of the Quohadi had been destroyed, hope for these people was at an end.

Appendix V

Oral Tradition and the Search for Factual Data Concerning Cynthia Ann Parker

A substantial body of data exists relating to the migration of the Parker family to Texas, the raid on Fort Parker, and the recapture of Cynthia Ann nearly a quarter of a century later. There are records of her final days and the attempt which was made to help her readjust to Anglo civilization by her white relatives. In addition, there is much information about Quanah and his leadership of the Comanche remnant as a reservation chief in Oklahoma.

However, there is no documentation concerning the twenty-four years that the Parker captive lived as a Quohadi. In order to gain an insight into the life of Cynthia Ann during her unknown years, it is necessary to put together the fragments of information which are available from a variety of sources.

Although the Indians did not deposit their records in state archives or send reports to commanding officers, generals, or national headquarters concerning their victories — or their defeats — they did preserve both historical data and cultural patterns through oral tradition. In many ways they were more conscious of their past than most who pride themselves on written history. They had a strong sense of continuum.

There are now several places where information about the unwritten history of the Comanche based on oral tradition are available. The Archives of Fort Sill contain records of a number of interviews with Comanches which have been carefully preserved in typescript form. In this repository there are also manuscripts and documents which constitute significant information both about Quanah Parker and his mother. This collection contains a vast storehouse of traditions relating to the Comanche culture due to the efforts of archivists who recorded interviews with Indians who had known life on the prairie prior to reservation days.

An extensive collection of papers also exists in the Panhandle-Plains Historical Museum, Canyon, Texas. The collected notes and papers of Bill Neeley have been preserved, along with various documents and photocopies of materials relating to the final days of the South Plains Indians on the prairie. This collection is of particular value since it has preserved a number of interviews with persons who were contemporary with the final demise of Comanche power.

In research involving Indian culture, interviews of this type, which reflect oral tradition, have considerable value. People such as the Comanches had to establish and maintain the same lifestyle for many generations. They were forced to continue traditions and procedures which had been successful in order to survive. Because they had little time for experimentation, identical cultural patterns would span centuries. Their fierce determination to hold on to the heritage of the past is apparent in conversations with modern descendants of the natives of Oklahoma and Texas.

In addition there are a number of firsthand accounts of the lifestyle of the Comanches during this period, such as the two accounts written by Rachel Plummer, and the extensive body of literature written by those who had lived as hostages among the Comanches: T. A. Babb, Jane Adeline Wilson, Ole T. Nystel, the Dollbeare account of Dolly Webster's captivity. These records of persons who had direct contact with Comanches during the middle years of the nineteenth century, along with studies of Comanche and Indian culture such as those by Newcomb and Fehrenbach, are important in determining what portion of the Cynthia Ann legend can be established as fact.

The search for factual data concerning Cynthia Ann Parker leads in a variety of directions.

The Texas State Archives in Austin is a significant source. A manuscript among the Lamar Papers gives a terse account of the raid on Fort Parker. There are other materials in the carefully preserved documents and publications which are a part of the state library holdings. The collection includes some contemporary firsthand accounts along with a variety of secondary sources.

Another important depository of materials contemporary with the Cynthia Ann story is that of the Barker Texas History Center at the University of Texas. A great deal of material is available there on Comanche culture, including several rare printed works written by persons who experienced captivity at the hands of the Plains Indians.

The National Archives in Washington, D.C., contains an extensive collection of letters, papers, and documents which represent the work of the Office (later Bureau) of Indian Affairs. This government agency was established in 1849 and was given general supervisory control of the Native American under the Department of the Interior.[1] This material is accessible on microfilm in the Archives Building in Washington.

There were brief references to Cynthia Ann in scholarly journals such as the *Southwestern Historical Quarterly*. A wide variety of other materials relating to her ranged all of the way from romantic fiction to serious efforts to determine factual data concerning her life.

One cannot explain or understand the saga of Cynthia Ann by considering only the documentation which is extant. After researching a variety of written materials, the author went to Oklahoma, talked to direct descendants of Cynthia Ann and Quanah, interviewed persons related to the story, both in Texas and in Oklahoma, visited actual sites where these events took place, and sought to secure as much information as possible about this beleaguered band of Comanches, their lifestyle, their people, and their existence.

It was then, and only then, that the full story of Cynthia Ann began to emerge.

Notes

I. May 19, 1836

1. One of the accounts of the raid on Fort Parker reported that the "ever faithful dog" of the Silas Parkers attacked an Indian horse. (Scarlett Kidd Bryant, *Under the Parker Tree*, 20) The details of the events of May 19, 1836, reported here are based on Bryant's record, which cites twelve Parker family authorities and the following contemporary accounts: Rachel Plummer's *Narrative*; the J. W. Parker Manuscript, in the Lamar Papers, Manuscript 2166 in the Texas State Archives; and Malcolm McLean's *Papers Concerning Robertson's Colony in Texas*, Volume X: 156.

2. The time sequence used in this account is based on Rachel Plummer's eyewitness description of the events of May 19, 1836 (Rachel Plummer, *Rachel Plummer's Narrative*, 6 ff.), upon her statement that her mistreatment lasted for half an hour and on the Parker family belief that the raiders appeared at the fort at 8:00 A.M.

3. Plummer, *op. cit.*, 6. Plummer's original record of her experiences as a captive was completed in September 1838, soon after her return to white civilization. She produced an enlarged edition of her original work, which she prepared for publication in December 1839. The 1839 version is available today as an appendix to James W. Parker's *The Rachel Plummer Narrative*.

4. Bryant reported that the men were both scalped and "mutilated." (Bryant, *op. cit.* 19) David Nevins' study of the conflict between white settlement and the natives of the plains reported that "Indians maimed the bodies of enemies in the belief that the slain men's spirits would then be identically crippled in the afterlife." (David Nevins, *The Old West: The Soldiers*, 17)

5. Plummer, *op. cit.*, 6.

6. Rachel Plummer's 1839 edition of the account of her sufferings stated that for her "to undertake to narrate their [the Indians'] barbarous treatment would only add to my present distress." (James W. Parker, *op.*

cit., 94) Later accounts discretely reported that the "women were molested." (Bryant, *op. cit.,* 19)

7. McLean, *op. cit.,* Volume X: 156.

8. The J. W. Parker Manuscript, The Lamar Papers, MS Number 2166, Texas State Archives, Austin, Texas.

9. *Loc. cit.*

10. Robert Goldthwaite Carter, *Tragedies of Canyon Blanco,* 8.

11. The Mack Boswell typescript in the Quanah Papers, Archives of Fort Sill, Oklahoma.

12. Plummer, *op. cit.,* 6, 7.

13. J. W. Parker, *op. cit.,* footnote to page 94.

14. Plummer, *op. cit.,* 6, 7.

15. The J. W. Parker Manuscript, The Lamar Papers, MS Number 2166, Texas State Archives, Austin, Texas.

16. Bryant, *op. cit.,* 20.

17. Plummer, *op. cit.,* 6.

18. *Loc. cit.*

19. The J. W. Parker Manuscript, The Lamar papers, MS Number 2166, Texas State Archives, Austin, Texas.

20. *Loc. cit.*

21. Bryant, *op. cit.,* 22.

22. *Loc. cit.*

23. Plummer, *op. cit.,* 7.

II. A Promised Land

1. Samuel Hessler, "Daniel Parker, 1781–1844 and the Establishment of the Pilgrim Church, 1833, the First Baptist Church in Texas," 13. (Typescript)

2. A typescript in the Quanah Papers in the Archives of Fort Sill, Oklahoma, stated that the winter of 1833–34 was a period of extreme inclemency.

3. Hessler, *op. cit.,* 13.

4. Bryant, *op. cit.,* 11.

5. One account placed the exploratory journey of the Parker brothers to Texas at a date early in 1831. However, the 1833 date for this trek would agree with other available information. (Hessler, *op. cit.,* 11)

6. Bryant, *op. cit.,* 11. The "Two-Seeds-in-the-Spirit" doctrine was an interpretation of Calvinism that held to the belief that the earthly generation of mankind produced two "seeds," a good one from God and a bad one from the devil. No change in this line of spiritual inheritance was believed to be possible.

7. Hessler, *op. cit.*, 8.

8. A typescript in the Quanah Papers, Archives of Fort Sill, Oklahoma.

9. This statement was recorded in a document among miscellaneous papers and clippings in the Quanah Papers, Archives of Fort Sill, Oklahoma.

10. Hessler, *op. cit.*, 3.

11. Manuscript letter signed by Daniel Parker, Manuscript Division of the Library of Congress, Washington, D.C., Box 186, 1821.

12. The Battle of Horseshoe Bend was also known by the Indian name "Tohopeka." Houston was wounded in the battle by a Creek arrow that had to be removed from his thigh.

13. Bryant, *op. cit.*, 9.

14. *Ibid.*, 4.

15. Hessler, *op. cit.*, 4.

16. *Ibid.*, 11.

17. Mirabeau Lamar described Texas in these words in his journal which he wrote about his trip to the Mexican province in 1835. (Phillip Graham, "Mirabeau Buonaparte Lamar's First Trip to Texas," *Southwest Review*, Volume 21, Number 4, 371)

18. Hessler, *op. cit.*, 11.

19. *Ibid.*, 12.

20. The Texas State Historical Commission marker near Palestine, Texas. Bryant's account stated that the full name of the congregation was "the Pilgrim Predestinarian Regular Baptist Church." (Bryant, *op. cit.*, 11)

21. Hessler, *op. cit.*, 13.

22. State Survey Commission Historical Marker near Palestine, Texas.

23. The Earnest Turney Manuscript in the Quanah Papers, Archives of Fort Sill, Oklahoma.

24. Bryant, *op. cit.*, 14.

25. Comanche oral tradition remembered the period immediately prior to the raid on Fort Parker as a time of severe storms during which there was "starvation and disease" among the Indians. (The Mack Boswell typescript in the Quanah Papers, Archives of Fort Sill, Oklahoma)

26. Bryant, *op. cit.*, 14.

III. The Forty Years War

1. Mirabeau Lamar described a gathering of settlers in his journal of his first trip to Texas in 1835 at which speakers called for a declaration of independence from Mexico. (Graham, *op. cit.*, 389)

2. Lewis Newton and Herbert Gambrell, *A Social and Political History of Texas*, 154.

3. Grace Jackson, *Cynthia Ann Parker*, 11.

4. Houston's report on the battle of San Jacinto has been recorded in Eugene Barker's article in the April, 1901 *Texas Historical Quarterly*; Santa Anna wrote his own account of the conflict which has been preserved in Castañeda's *The Mexican Side of the Texas Revolution*. 176 ff.

5. Bryant, *op. cit.*, 14.

6. A manuscript letter signed "T.B.A" written in the mid-nineteenth century spoke of Indians who "have fine land around them" which they did not cultivate. (Manuscript Department of the University of North Carolina Library, Number 733)

7. Ernest Wallace and E. Adamson Hoebel, in their study of the Texan-Comanche conflict, recognized that the raid on Fort Parker initiated full-scale warfare: "The year 1835 marks the beginning of hostile raids against the Anglo-American settlements in Texas." In referring to the capture of Cynthia Ann, they reported: "A group of Northern Comanches and their Kiowa allies made a destructive raid on the Texas frontier in May, 1836." Wallace and Hoebel, *The Comanches: Lords of the South Plains*, 292)

IV. Captive Journey

1. Bryant, *op. cit.*, 19.

2. Plummer, *op. cit.*, 6.

3. The Pioneer Monument at Groesbeck, Texas.

4. J. W. Wilbarger, *Indian Depredations in Texas*, 20.

5. Plummer, *op. cit.*, 6.

6. *Ibid.*, 7.

7. Ole Nystel, who was a captive of the Comanches during this same period, believed he had been selected for integration into a Comanche tribe. (Ole Nystel, *Lost and Found or Three Months with the Wild Indians*, 14) T. A. Babb, another young captive who lived for a time among the Comanches, indicated in his record of captivity that he was a candidate for acceptance into the tribe. (T. A. Babb, *In the Bosom of the Comanches*, 132 ff.)

8. Comanches on the trail "wore very little clothing or nothing at all." (An interview with Cassie Suggs Brown, recorded in a typescript in

the Panhandle-Plains Historical Museum Research Center, Canyon, Texas)

9. Benjamin Dollbeare, *A Narrative of the Captivity and Suffering of Dolly Webster Among the Camanche* [sic] *Indians of Texas*, 10.

10. Nystel, *op. cit.*, 11.

11. *Loc. cit.*

12. *Ibid.*, 11.

13. Plummer, *op. cit.*, 9.

14. *Ibid.*, 7.

15. *Loc. cit.*

16. The J. W. Parker Manuscript, The Lamar Papers, Manuscript 2166, Texas State Archives, Austin, Texas.

17. Plummer, *op. cit.*, 9.

18. Several variations of the spelling of the tribal name "Quohadi" have appeared in print, any one of which would be a possible interpretation of the sound of the spoken word. This spelling has been adopted here for consistency.

19. Plummer, *op. cit.*, 9.

20. *Loc. cit.*

21. *Loc. cit.*

22. Plummer, *op. cit.*, 11.

23. Dollbeare, *op. cit.*, 9.

24. Plummer, *op. cit.*, 10.

25. *Ibid.*, 11, 12.

26. *Ibid.*, 13.

27. *Ibid.*, 15.

28. *Loc. cit.*

29. The J. W. Parker Manuscript, the Lamar Papers, Manuscript Number 2166, Texas State Archives, Austin, Texas.

30. *Loc. cit.*

V. Sinthy Ann Remains

1. The Lamar Papers, Manuscript Number 392, Texas State Archives, Austin, Texas.

2. The Lamar Papers, Manuscript Number 414, Texas State Archives, Austin, Texas.

3. The Lamar Papers, Manuscript Number 427, Texas State Archives, Austin, Texas.

4. The J. W. Parker Manuscript, the Lamar Papers, Manuscript Number 2166, Texas State Archives, Austin, Texas.

5. Plummer, *op. cit.*, 15.

6. A. K. Christian, "Mirabeau B. Lamar," *Southwestern Historical Quarterly*, Volume 24:245.

7. Mary Whatley Clarke, *Chief Bowles and the Texas Cherokees*, 52.

8. Christian, *op. cit.*, 53 ff.

9. Mary Whatley Clarke, *op. cit.*, 52.

10. The first edition of Rachel Plummer's *Narrative* was dated September 23, 1838, in which she declared "I have written this narrative partly in Santa Fe and partly in Missouri and completed it at my father's house in Texas." (Plummer, *op. cit.*, Preface)

11. The Lamar Papers, Manuscripts 995 and 1100, Texas State Archives, Austin, Texas.

12. "Letter of His Excellency the President to Col. Bowles and Others" (Photostat), 3, Texas State Archives, Austin, Texas.

13. The Lamar Papers, Manuscripts 1372 and 1373, Texas State Archives, Austin, Texas.

14. The Lamar Papers, Manuscript Number 1855, Texas State Archives, Austin, Texas.

15. The Lamar Papers, Manuscript Number 1863, Texas State Archives, Austin, Texas.

16. Victor Lee James, *Frontier and Pioneer Recollections of Early Days in San Antonio and West Texas*, 24.

17. Rupert N. Richardson, *The Comanche Barrier to South Plains Settlement*, footnote to page 91. A document in the Quanah Papers in the Archives of Fort Sill, Oklahoma, dated this event as occurring during the year 1840.

18. Richardson, *op. cit.*, footnote to page 91.

19. The James W. Parker Manuscript, The Lamar Papers, Manuscript Number 2166, Texas State Archives, Austin, Texas.

20. A typescript in the Quanah Papers, Archives of Fort Sill, Oklahoma.

21. The Dorothy Dale typescript entitled "The Parker Family" in the Quanah Papers, Archives of Fort Sill, Oklahoma, gave December 3, 1844, as the date of Daniel Parker's death.

22. Richardson, *op. cit.*, footnote to page 91.

VI. A TROPHY OF CONQUEST

1. The author traveled the general route which Cynthia Ann's captors would have taken on this trek following as closely as modern means of transportation would allow in May 1987.

2. W. L. Marcy, *U.S. Bureau of Indian Affairs, Texas Indians, 29th Congress, Second Session, Document Number 76*, 6.

3. The account of T. A. Babb, who was a Comanche captive during this same period, provides an important clue to why Cynthia Ann was so readily accepted into the Quohadi tribe. He stated that the South Plains nomads believed their own women to be less prolific than their Anglo counterparts. (Babb, *op. cit.*, 142) As a matter of fact, many of the early settlers on the frontier did have large families. Mirabeau Lamar recorded in his journal that, during his first trip to Texas, he spent the night in the home of a family which had produced twenty-five children. This, he declared, was certainly "a praiseworthy effort to settle the southwestern wilds." (Graham, *op. cit.*, 356)

4. Babb, *op. cit.* 142.

5. Fannie McAlpine Clark, "A Chapter in the Life of a Young Territory," *Texas Historical Association Quarterly*, Volume 9: 59.

6. Plummer, *op. cit.*, 13.

7. Manuscript notes in the Neeley Papers in the Panhandle-Plains Historical Museum, Canyon, Texas.

8. House, *A Narrative of the Capture of Mrs. Horn and her Two Children with that of Mrs. Harris by the Camanche* [sic] *Indians*, 35; Nystel, *op. cit.*, 11.

9. Nystel published two accounts of his experiences as a Comanche: *Lost and Found* and *From Bondage to Freedom*.

10. Babb recounted his experiences in his work previously cited, *In the Bosom of the Comanches*.

11. Nelson Lee's record of his experiences while living with a South Plains tribe was published under the title, *Three Years Among the Comanches*.

12. See Appendix III.

13. Jane Adeline Wilson's experiences were first published in 1853 under the title, *A Thrillinq Narrative of the Sufferinqs of Mrs. Jane Adeline Wilson During Her Captivitv Among the Comanche Indians*.

14. E. House, *A Narrative of the Captivitv of Mrs. Horn and her Two Children with that of Mrs. Harris by the Camanche* [sic] *Indians*, a work which was published in 1839.

15. E. House, *op. cit.*, 35.

16. Wilson, *op. cit.*, 17–19.

17. Clark Wissler, *North American Indians of the Plains*, 162.

18. W. W. Newcomb, Jr., *The Indians of Texas: From Prehistoric to Modern Times*, 160.

19. A typescript in the Quanah Papers, Archives of Fort Sill, Oklahoma.

20. The Quanah Papers in the Archives of Fort Sill, Oklahoma.

21. House Document Number 76, Second Session, 29th Congress, 8.

22. A. E. Butterfield, *Comanche, Kiowa and Apache Missions*, 13.

23. R. B. Marcy, *Adventures on the Red River*, 169.

24. Dollbeare, *op. cit.,* 11.

25. Nystel, *op. cit.,* 11 ff.

26. R. B. Marcy, *Thirty Years of Army Life,* 49.

27. An unsigned manuscript in the Quanah Papers, Archives of Fort Sill, Oklahoma.

28. Nystel, *op. cit.,* 19.

29. An unsigned manuscript in the Quanah Papers, Archives of Fort Sill, Oklahoma.

30. R. B. Marcy, *Exploration of the Red River,* 103.

31. Comanche tradition contends that Cynthia Ann was the primary wife of Peta Nocona. When an aged Indian named Mam-sook-a-wyt questioned this fact in an interview in 1930 casting doubt on the ancestry of Quanah, he was declared to be a renegade and later was refused burial in the tribal cemetery. (A typescript dated July 1930 in the Quanah Papers, Archives of Fort Sill, Oklahoma)

32. A typescript in the Quanah Papers, Archives of Fort Sill, Oklahoma.

33. This interpretation of the meaning of the name Quanah was given to the author by descendants of the Comanche chief in an interview in May 1986. See Appendix II for a discussion of the date of Quanah's birth.

34. A manuscript letter in the Quanah Papers, Archives of Fort Sill, Oklahoma. See Appendix II.

35. The name Pecos means "Peanut." It is likely that Cynthia Ann's second son was named for the river which was an important geographical feature of the Comanche range rather than for the small nut which grows in the vicinity of the Pecos River.

36. Dollbeare, *op. cit.,* 11.

37. Interview with descendants of Quanah Parker in Cache, Oklahoma, May 1986. See Appendix IV.

38. Larry Barness, *Heads, Hides and Horns,* 106. Comanche warriors rode bareback, but women of the tribe were allowed light saddles.

39. Wissler, *op. cit.,* 162.

40. Babb, *op. cit.,* 132. In May 1986, the author was shown a tepee which Comanche descendants had erected near Cache, Oklahoma. Lodge poles which had survived from pre-reservation days were used in the structure. The owners, who were proud they had been able to preserve this portion of their past, apologized that painted plastic had to be placed over the poles in lieu of buffalo hides.

VII. THE UNSPOKEN NEGATIVE

1. Newton and Gambrell, *op. cit.*, 232.

2. The Lamar Papers, Manuscripts 2211, 2212, and 2216, Texas State Archives.

3. In the spring of 1846, an American army under Gen. Zachary Taylor moved to the mouth of the Rio Grande in order to blockade the city of Matamoros. This action precipitated an attack by Mexican forces on April 25, an event which was used as a provocation for the declaration of war against Mexico. Taylor then proceeded inland during the summer of 1846 to attack the city of Monterrey.

4. Bryant, *op. cit.*, 27.

5. Several years after his return to white civilization, John Parker told R. B. Marcy that he had visited Cynthia Ann and had personally urged her to return to her natal family. (Richardson, *op. cit.*, footnote to page 91)

6. Bryant, *op. cit.*, 26.

7. James T. DeShields, *Cynthia Ann Parker: The Story of Her Capture*, 30. Another record of this event gave the name of one of the traders as a "Mr. Stout." (A document in the Quanah Papers, Archives of Fort Sill, Oklahoma)

8. Jackson, *op. cit.*, vii.

9. Hugh Corwin, *Comanche and Kiowa Captives*, 38.

10. R. B. Marcy, *Adventures on the Red River*, xiii.

11. *Ibid.*, 169.

12. House Document Number 76, Second Session, 29th Congress, 8 (Letter from P. M. Butler and M. G. Lewis, Indian Commissioners, to W. Medill, Commissioner of Indian Affairs, Washington City, D.C. — August 8, 1846)

13. Bryant, *op. cit.*, 27; DeShields, *op. cit.*, 32. This could have been a retelling of the encounter described by the Stoal and Williams party. However, since "children" were mentioned, this would have taken place after the birth of both Quanah and Pecos, a fact which would place this event at about the year 1850.

14. Charles Sommer, *Quanah Parker: Last Chief of the Comanches*, 7.

15. Wilbarger, *op. cit.*, 317.

16. The United States Bureau of Indian Affairs in a report on Texas Indians gave the tribal name of these people as "Nocoonees" meaning "people in a circle." (*Texas Indians, 29th Congress, Second Session, Document Number 76, Report of Secretary of War W. L. Marcy*, 6)

17. One account of life among the Comanches, based on the recollections of two brothers, Clinton and Jeff Smith, who had been captured by

South Plains nomads, stated that their "ramblings carried them into the Rocky Mountains and even to the Pacific coast." (J. Marvin Hunter, *The Boy Captives*, 6, 7) It is worth noting that the claim they were carried as far as the Pacific was made years after the event: the truth behind such a claim would be the fact that Comanche nomads did travel great distances ranging throughout the Southwest and into northern Mexico.

18. W. B. Parker, *Notes Taken During the Expedition Commanded by Capt. R. B. Marcy, USA, Through Unexplored Texas in the Summer and Fall of 1854*, ix.

19. R. B. Marcy's account of this expedition was published under the title *The Prairie Traveler, A Hand-book for Overland Expeditions*.

20. W. B. Parker, *op. cit.* 188.

VIII. No Word For Home

1. Peter Gallagher, *The Santa Fe Expedition*, 23. Several accounts of the Texas Santa Fe Expedition are extant. In addition to Gallagher's diary, other members of the trek wrote detailed accounts. George Kendall of the New Orleans *Picayune* and Thomas Falconer, an English journalist, also accompanied the entourage and published records of the journey. (Kendall, *Narrative of the Texas Santa Fe Expedition;* Falconer, *Letters and Notes on the Texas Santa Fe Expedition, 1841–1842*) *Another contemporary narration of the expedition was authored by Stephen Holye entitled Journal of the Santa Fe Expedition.*

2. Gallagher, *op. cit.*, 21, 22.

3. *Ibid.*, 23.

4. A typescript containing information attributed to Charles Goodnight in Quanah Papers in the Panhandle-Plains Historical Museum, Canyon, Texas.

5. Corwin, *op. cit.*, 31 and Map Number 3.

6. Gallagher, *op. cit.* 26, 27.

7. A typescript in the Quanah Papers in the Panhandle-Plains Historical Museum, Canyon, Texas.

8. Gallagher, *op. cit.*, 30.

9. *Loc. cit.*

10. *Ibid.*, 42.

11. J. Evetts Haley, "Focus on the Frontier," *The Shamrock*, Spring 1957.

12. Wayne Gard, "The Mooar Brothers, Buffalo Hunters," *Southwestern Historical Quarterly*, Volume 63:31.

13. Carter, *op. cit.*, 4.

14. C. R. Wharton, *The Baron of Bastrop*, 8.

15. J. Evetts Haley, *Fort Concho and the Texas Frontier*, 15.

16. Butterfield, *op. cit.*, 23.
17. Newcomb, *op. cit.*, 160.
18. Wilcomb E. Washburn, *The Indian in America*, 44.
19. Fannie McAlpine Clark, *op. cit.*, 59.
20. The Lamar Papers, Manuscripts 1863 and 1874, Texas State Archives, Austin, Texas.
21. A typescript of an interview with Herman Asanap, October 30, 1937, in the Quanah Papers in the Panhandle-Plains Historical Museum, Canyon, Texas.
22. Joseph H. Cash and Gerald W. Wolff, *The Comanche People*,
23. Butterfield, *op. cit.*, 23.

IX. THE TURNING POINT

1. J. W. Williams, "The Van Dorn Trails," *Southwestern Historical Quarterly*, Volume 44:321; Walter Prescott Webb, *The Story of the Texas Rangers*, 27.
2. Thomas Robert Havins, *Beyond the Cimarron: Major Earl Van Dorn in Comanche Land*, 71.
3. Williams, *op. cit.*, 326.
4. The location of the boundary between Texas and Oklahoma territory was in dispute at the time, a question which was not settled by litigation until the twentieth century. (*Texas Bar Journal*, Volume 50, Number 11, 1218) However, Ford and his men were prepared to hunt down their enemy regardless of whether or not they believed themselves to be on federal land.
5. Webb, *op. cit.*, 27.
6. *Loc. cit.*
7. Wilbarger, *op. cit.*, 320.
8. *Ibid.*, 322.
9. Although this battle has been referred to as "The Battle of Antelope Hills" (Jackson, *op. cit.*, 70), early maps, such as the Colton Map of Texas published in 1873, show only a single prominence, a high elevation on the south side of the Canadian River, near which the battle took place.
10. George E. Hyde, *Rangers and Regulars*, 81.
11. Wilbarger, *op. cit.*, 322. Walter Prescott Webb raised a doubt about the size of Quasho's force, commenting simply that Ford and his men "killed seventy-six Indians." (Webb, *op. cit.*, 27)
12. Wilbarger, *op. cit.*, 321 ff.
13. Havins, *op. cit.*, 71.
14. Hyde, *op. cit.*, 81.
15. Wilbarger, *op. cit.*, 323.

16. Hyde, *op. cit.*, 82.

17. *Ibid.*, 83.

18. Wilbarger, *op. cit.*, 324.

19. *Ibid.*, 325. It is doubtful that the Comanche warriors led by Quasho ever numbered as many as 400.

20. DeShields, *op. cit.*, 41.

21. Willbarger, *op. cit.*, 325.

22. DeShields, *op. cit.*, 43; Hyde, *op. cit.*, 83.

23. Hyde, *op. cit.*, 83.

24. DeShields, *op. cit.*, 83.

25. Wilbarger, *op. cit.*, 325.

26. Hyde, *op. cit.*, 84.

27. *Ibid.*, 83.

28. *Ibid.*, 84. Several Spanish coats of mail were believed to be in existence during the middle years of the nineteenth century probably bartered by New Mexicans who traded with the Plains Indians. Apparently Quasho had possession of one of these, and used it to promote his claim of immunity to death in battle. One account stated that the iron shirt was taken back to Austin as a trophy by members of Ford's command. (Douglas, *Gentlemen in White Hats*, 53)

29. Williams, *op. cit.*, 326.

30. Webb, *op. cit.*, 26–29.

31. Dee Brown, in a history of the Indians of the American West, cited the United States Bureau of Ethnology (Report, 14th, 18921893, Part 2, 789) in declaring that "of the 3,700,000 buffalo destroyed from 1872 through 1874, only 150,000 were killed by Indians." General Sheridan envisioned the total destruction of the buffalo as "the only way to bring lasting peace" to the frontier. (Brown, *Bury My Heart at Wounded Knee*, 254)

32. A typescript prepared by Morris Swett in the Archives of Fort Sill, Oklahoma, estimated that the Comanches numbered in excess of 7,000 during the early years of the nineteenth century. He reported that by the beginning of the twentieth century their numbers had dropped to no more than 1,400. Another authority, Benjamin Capps, believed that the Comanches numbered as many as 10,000 persons in the year 1840. (Benjamin Capps, *The Old West: The Indians*, 24)

33. Washburn, *op. cit.*, 157.

34. A typescript by Morris Swett in the Quanah Papers, Archives of Fort Sill, Oklahoma.

35. Douglas, *op. cit.*, 56.

36. Hyde, *op. cit.*, 86.

37. Nye, *Carbine and Lance*, 27–29.

38. *Ibid.*, 62.

39. Williams, *op. cit.*, 327.

40. The Armand Soubie Papers include a series of letters written by Charles Hummel to an arms supplier in New Orleans relating to the shipment of large quantities of small arms to Texas. The letters are dated 1854 through 1857. During the later part of this period, large quantities of weapons were shipped described as "belt pistoles," "pistoles de Colt," and "Navy pistols." These were sold by Hummel to individuals in Texas who were anxious to protect themselves and their families from raids by Comanche Indians. (Armand Soubie Papers, Manuscript Department of the University of North Carolina Library, Accession Number 3031)

41. James Buchanan, *Message from the President of the United States, Difficulties on the Southwestern Frontier*, 15, 16.

42. *Loc. cit.*

43. Havins, *op. cit.*, 102.

44. Hyde, *op. cit.*, 69.

45. *Ibid*, 70.

46. The National Archives, Records of the Office of Indian Affairs, Letters Sent, 59:7.

47. *Loc. cit.*

48. Hyde, *op. cit.*, 71.

49. David Agee Horr, editor, *Kiowa-Commanche* [sic] *Indian Transcripts of Hearings of the Kiowa, Comanche, and Apache Tribes of Indians vs. the United States of America*, 83, 84.

50. These words were spoken by Abraham Lincoln in the opening speech of his campaign for election to the Senate on June 17, 1858. (Cited by Samuel E. Morrison and Henry Steele Commager, *The Growth of the American Republic*, 1:628.

51. The Mack Boswell typescript in the Quanah Papers, Archives of Fort Sill, Oklahoma, 2.

X. SUNSET ON THE PRAIRIE

1. An interview with Dick Banks in 1938 recorded in the Quanah Papers, Panhandle-Plains Historical Museum, Canyon, Texas. See Appendix IV.

2. Douglas, *op. cit.*, 56.

3. Carl Waldman, *Atlas of the North American Indian*, 57.

4. See Appendix IV.

5. Nystel, *op. cit.*, 9.

6. See Appendix IV.

7. Daniel A. Becker, "Comanche Civilization With the History of Quanah Parker," *Chronicles of Oklahoma*, 1:252.

8. Interview with members of the Native American Church, June 16, 1987. See Appendix IV.

9. David E. Jones, *Sanapia: Comanche Medicine Woman,* ix.

10. Manuscript notes in the Quanah Papers, Panhandle-Plains Historical Museum, Canyon, Texas.

11. Cash and Wolff, *op. cit.,* 28.

12. J'Nell Pate, *Great Plains Journal,* Volume 16, Number 1, 16.

13. Benjamin Capps quotes an Indian named Eagle Chief, a leader of the Skidi band of Pawnees, as the authority for describing a ceremony such as this in which the victim was sacrificed to the Indian god Tirawa. (Capps, *op. cit.,* 123, 124.

14. See Appendix IV.

15. The name Topsannah or Toh-tsee-ah meant "flower" or "flower of the prairie." (The Quanah Papers, Archives of Fort Sill, Oklahoma)

16. A typescript in the Quanah Papers, Fort Sill Archives, Oklahoma, quotes the statement by Quanah in which he spoke of "two sisters." There is no other evidence of a second daughter of Cynthia Ann. Quanah probably considered the young Quohadi girl who was gunned down in the 1860 raid a sister. It is more likely, however, that she was a younger wife of Peta Nocona.

17. A typescript quoting Wanda Page in the Quanah Papers, Archives of Fort Sill, Oklahoma.

18. A typescript by Morris Swett in the Quanah Papers, Archives of Fort Sill, Oklahoma.

19. J. Evetts Haley, *Charles Goodnight's Recollections,* 15.

20. Fannie McAlpine Clark, *op. cit.,* 58.

XI. THE RECAPTURE

1. Fannie McAlpine Clark, *op. cit.,* 59 ff.

2. Ross believed he had killed the Comanche chief. Other members of his ranger company were certain they had witnessed the death of Nocona. (DeShields, *op. cit.,* 50 ff) However, after Quanah had led his people to the reservation, the son of Cynthia Ann and Nocona insisted that his father had survived the attack on the Quohadi and had lived for several years after the recapture of Cynthia Ann. See Appendix I.

3. A manuscript record in the Panhandle-Plains Historical Museum, Canyon, Texas, to which was appended a note declaring that this statement was "dictated to J. Evetts Haley, November 13, 1926 by Charles Goodnight."

4. George Hyde, in a work which was based on information gained from Indian eyewitnesses to the final days of Indian warfare, stated No-

cona escaped death in the Ross raid and fought against a ranger company a year later. (Hyde, *op. cit.*, 94)

5. Mildred Mayhall, in her critique of Jackson's account of the life of Cynthia Ann, declared that the ranger assault was merely "an attack upon a camp of women, children and slaves who were gathering, drying and loading meat for winter use. No Indian braves were present." (Mildred Mayhall, *Southwestern Historical Quarterly*, 64:282) However, given the weather conditions and the time of the year, it is hard to accept the assumption that all of the tribal warriors were either on an extended hunt or seeking to do battle with a distant tribe. The Quohadi would not have left a major encampment undefended. It is much more likely that at least some of the fighting men were present at the time. The Gholson account of the battle (*Southwestern Historical Quarterly*, 46:18) indicated that the rangers believed they were fighting Comanche warriors. DeShield's information, which he claimed had been provided by those who were present at the conflict, would agree with this conclusion. (DeShields, *op. cit.*, preface to the 1886 edition)

6. A grandson of Quanah Parker, in an interview granted the author, repeatedly affirmed the family belief that Nocona was not present at the time of the raid. It was his conviction that both Quanah and his father were in the Wichita Mountains when Ross raided the camp. (Interview, May 1986, Cache, Oklahoma)

7. Wanda Page, a descendant of Quanah, stated that the person killed who was thought to be Nocona was "Cynthia Ann's personal servant" who "was a Mexican captive." (The Wanda Page manuscript in the Quanah Papers, Archives of Fort Sill, Oklahoma) Morris Swett quoted Quanah as having said that the Mexican who died at the hands of the rangers was "Yaqua, the body guard of Cynthia Ann." (The Morris Swett typescript in the Quanah Papers, Archives of Fort Sill, Oklahoma)

8. Ross later reported he was able to distinguish the captive as white from the fact that beneath the Comanche garb and the suntanned face, he could see blue eyes, a characteristic not known among Indians. (Fannie McAlpine Clark, *op. cit.*, 59)

9. A typescript in the Dixon Papers, Panhandle-Plains Historical Museum, Canyon, Texas.

10. Carter, *op. cit.*, 13.

11. Succession of a son to his father's position as chief of a tribe was not automatic. The fact that Quanah was the son of Peta Nocona did not guarantee he would become chief of the Quohadi or any other band of Indians: it was necessary for him to prove himself in some fashion before his leadership would be accepted. Certainly he did not reach the status of principal chief until after the time in which he was influential in leading

the last of the Comanches to reservation. (Pate, *op. cit.*, 19; Charles Sommer, *op. cit.* 11)

12. Judith Ann Benner, *Sul Ross: Soldier, Statesman, Educator*, 56.

13. Jack Loftin, *Trails Through Archer*, 60.

14. Isaac Parker was a member of the Texas State Senate in 1860 and was active in the secession movement. He died in April 1883. (Typescript in the Quanah Papers, Archives of Fort Sill, Oklahoma)

15. One account stated that Cynthia Ann "could not speak English" at the time of her recapture. ("Biographies of Leading Texans," a typescript in the Texas State Archives, 3:580) Probably her silence was due as much to her distrust of those who had forcibly removed her from her life as a Quohadi as to the fact she had forgotten much of the language she had known as a young girl.

16. Pauline Buck Hohes, *Centennial History of Anderson County*, 26.

17. "Biographies of Leading Texans," typescript, Texas State Archives, 3:580.

18. The Senate Journal of the Ninth Legislature of Texas included the following record: "Bill amendatory of an act and supplemental to the second section of an Act granting pension to Cynthia Ann Parker, Approved April 8, 1861." (James M. Day, editor, *Senate Journal of the Ninth Legislature of the State of Texas, Regular Session, November 4, 1861–January 14, 1862*, 209)

19. Bryant, *op. cit.*, 30. G. A. Holland, in commenting on Cynthia Ann's desire to return to her Quohadi people, stated: "After years of such companionable, unrestricted freedom, it is no wonder that she was not satisfied and wanted to return to the nomadic life." (G. A. Holland, *History of Parker Country and the Double Log Cabin*, 53)

20. Bryant, *op. cit.*, 30.

21. Carl Coke Rister, *Border Captives*, 83.

22. *Loc. cit.*

23. Bryant, *op. cit.*, 30.

24. Coho Smith, *Cohographs*, 69–71.

25. *Ibid.*, 72.

26. Bryant, *op. cit.*, 31.

27. A letter from Annie and John Milner to E. O'Quinn stated that a grandmother, Elma Scarborough, could remember that her "mother played with Cynthia Ann and helped her relearn the English language." (Photocopy in the Quanah Papers, Archives of Fort Sill, Oklahoma)

28. Some accounts have assumed that Topsannah died during the period that Cynthia Ann lived with the Silas Mercer Parker, Jr. family in Van Zandt County. This assumption was based on the fact that the family believed the infant's grave was located near the Parker residence. How-

ever, A. C. Birdsong produced a notarized statement declaring that he had found both graves near the O'Quinn home in Anderson County and that he added the bones of the child to those of the mother when he shipped them to Oklahoma for reburial. (A typescript signed by A. C. Birdsong in the Quanah Papers, Archives of Fort Sill, Oklahoma)

29. Bryant, *op. cit.*, 31.

30. Marian T. Place, *Comanches and Other Indians of Texas,* 87.

31. The gravestone of Cynthia Ann Parker in the Fort Sill Post Cemetery gives the date 1870 as the year of her death. However, most evidence points to an earlier date. Information in the possession of the descendants of Quanah in Cache, Oklahoma, reported 1864 as the date of her death. Scarlett Bryant's paper,
based on Parker family sources, stated that "Cynthia Ann Parker died October 28, 1864, while living with her sister." (Bryant, *op. cit.*, 31) Probably Topsannah's death occurred early in 1864 and the mother's death took place in the fall of that same year. The fact that both bodies were buried in Anderson County would further support the probability that both deaths took place within a period of less than twelve months. (A. C. Birdsong typescript in the Quanah Papers, Archives of Fort Sill, Oklahoma)

XII. TIGHTENING THE NOOSE

1. See Appendix I.

2. The Lamar Papers, Manuscript Number 1863, Texas State Archives, Austin, Texas.

3. The Morris Swett typescript, the Quanah Papers, Archives of Fort Sill, Oklahoma.

4. Newcomb, *op. cit.,* 161.

5. *Loc. cit.*

6. Nevins, *op. cit.,* 22, 23.

7. Nevins stated that "some scholars" believe "since the buffalo was a sacred animal, the Indians honored the Blacks" by applying the name "Buffalo soldier" to them. (Nevins, *op. cit.,* 25)

8. Edward E. Hill, *American Indians,* 296.

9. *Loc. cit.*

10. Carter, *op. cit.,* 6 ff.

11. Pate, *op. cit.,* 20 ff.

12. Wayne Gard stated in referring to the impact of the buffalo hunter upon the Comanche that "by depriving the hostile Plains Indian of his chief source of food, garb and shelter, he [was] starved into submission." (Wayne Gard, *op. cit.,* 31)

XIII. The Reunion

1. See Appendix II for a discussion of the date and the site of Quanah's birth.

2. Charles Sommer, *op. cit.* 11, 18.

3. A typescript of a speech by Quanah dated July 1896, in the Quanah Papers, Archives of Fort Sill, Oklahoma.

4. Newcomb, *op. cit.*, 362.

5. William T. Hagan, *United States-Comanche Relations*, 1.

6. Carter, *op. cit.*, 6.

7. Charles Sommer, *op. cit.*, 20 ff.

8. T. R. Fehrenbach, *Comanches: The Destruction of a People*, 513.

9. Paul Foreman, *Quanah: The Serpent Eagle*, 104.

10. J. Evetts Haley, *Fort Concho and the Texas Frontier*, 183 ff.

11. *Ibid.*, 186.

12. The author explored the Soldier's Mound area in 1987 and discovered the north slope which was probably used by Mackenzie's troops as a defendable access. All other sides of the mound still rise steeply 150 feet or more above the nearby fields in spite of extensive quarrying in recent years that has removed some of this natural phenomenon's dramatic rock formations. The height of the elevation gave the occupants clear visibility of the surrounding territory.

13. A typescript in the Quanah Papers, Panhandle-Plains Historical Museum, Canyon, Texas.

14. A typescript in the Quanah Papers which dated the incident in which the Comanche chief captured the cavalry commander's mount as October 10, 1871, in the Archives of Fort Sill, Oklahoma.

15. Wilcomb E. Washburn, *The American Indian and the United States: A Documentary History*, 1:182.

16. Typescript by Wayne Parker in the Quanah Papers, Panhandle-Plains Historical Museum, Canyon, Texas.

17. Charles Sommer, *op. cit.*, 22.

18. A typescript by A. C. Birdsong in the Quanah Papers, Archives of Fort Sill, Oklahoma.

19. DeShields, *op. cit.*, 66 ff.

20. A typescript by A. C. Birdsong in the Quanah Papers, Archives of Fort Sill, Oklahoma.

21. *Loc. cit.*

22. Joe F. Taylor, compiler, *The Indian Campaign on the Staked Plains, 1874–1875: Military Correspondence from War Department Adjutant General's Office, File 2815 — 1874, 141.*

23. *R. David Edmunds, editor, Studies in Diversity: American Indian Leaders,* 176.

24. *Ibid.,* 185.

25. *Ibid.,* 189.

26. Charles Sommer, *op. cit.,* 36.

27. Edmunds, editor, *op. cit.,* 176.

28. DeShields, *op. cit.,* 76 ff.

29. The gas light incident was recorded in a report of an interview with George W. Biggs in the Quanah Papers, Panhandle-Plains Historical Museum, Canyon, Texas.

30. Charles Sommer, *op. cit.,* 39.

31. The residence built by Quanah Parker was visited by the author in 1986 at the site in Cache, Oklahoma, to which it had been moved when the portion of the reservation upon which it had originally been built was reclaimed as government land. The four stars could still be seen on the roof, appearing from the ground to be upside down; however, the painter, who worked from the top of the roof, saw them as properly positioned. When Quanah knew he was near death, he asked to be carried back to this building in which he had lived for many years with his several wives, each of whom had her own bedroom and area of importance in the large dwelling.

32. One account, taken from a recorded interview with J. J. Methwin and H. M. Lindsay conducted by Lillian Gassaway in 1937, stated that Quanah had a total of twelve wives. However, he probably never had more than seven at any one time. (The Quanah Papers, Panhandle-Plains Historical Museum, Canyon, Texas)

33. Albert S. Gilles, Sr., *Comanche Days,* 40, 41.

34. Edmunds, editor, *op. cit.,* 188.

35. *Ibid., 293.*

36. *A manuscript reporting a statement by Charles Goodnight in the Quanah Papers, Panhandle-Plains Historical Museum, Canyon, Texas.*

37. *A manuscript of an interview in 1941 in the Quanah Papers in the Panhandle-Plains Historical Museum, Canyon, Texas.*

38. *An interview conducted by Bessie Thomas with Lena R. Banks of Cache, Oklahoma, in 1938 recorded in the Quanah Papers, Panhandle-Plains Historical Museum, Canyon, Texas.*

39. *A typescript in the Dixon Papers, Panhandle-Plains Historical Museum, Canyon, Texas.*

40. *A typescript in the Quanah Papers, Archives of Fort Sill, Oklahoma.*

41. *Waldman, op. cit.,* 153.

42. William Hagan in his study of the life of Quanah stated that he "probably introduced the Comanches to peyote; certainly he was a leader in the peyote cult." (David Edmunds, editor, *op. cit.,* 186) The testimony

from Sanapia, however, would indicate that the use of the drug had been a part of the culture of the South Plains Indians for centuries. (David Jones, *op. cit.*, 78 ff.)

43. A letter dated February 28, 1907, from the Wormser Brothers, Laredo, Texas, addressed to Quanah in the Quanah Papers, Archives of Fort Sill, Oklahoma.

44. Interview with J. J. Methwin by Lillian Gassaway, December 1937, recorded in the Quanah Papers, Panhandle-Plains Historical Museum, Canyon, Texas.

45. Wilcomb E. Washburn, *The Indian in America*. 242.

46. Waldman, *op. cit.*, 153.

47. Interviews with members of the Native American Church during the Peyote Trial in the Federal Court Building, Dallas, Texas, June 16, 1987. See Appendix IV.

48. The bedroom in which Quanah was reported to have died in the Star House in Cache, Oklahoma, includes among its furnishings a copy of the photograph of Cynthia Ann and Topsannah, which was made in Fort Worth in 1861.

49. A manuscript letter dated June 19, 1908, signed by J. R. O'Quinn of Rio Vista, Texas, in the Quanah Papers, Archives of Fort Sill, Oklahoma.

50. A manuscript signed by A. C. Birdsong in the Quanah Papers, Archives of Fort Sill, Oklahoma.

51. Interview with Knox Beal by R. B. Thomas in 1937 recorded in the Quanah Papers, Panhandle-Plains Historical Museum, Canyon, Texas.

52. A manuscript in the Quanah Papers, Archives of Fort Sill, Oklahoma.

53. This statement is included in a notarized typescript signed by A. C. Birdsong dated September 2, 1956, in the Quanah Papers, Archives of Fort Sill, Oklahoma. Birdsong prepared this document in answer to a claim which had been made that the remains of Topsannah were buried in Asbury Cemetery, near Edon, Van Zandt County. On August 25, 1965, the Texas Department of Health issued a disinterment permit for opening what was believed by some to be the grave of Cynthia Ann's daughter. However, on October 2, 1965, Stan Redding of the Texas Rangers reported on the effort to find and remove the body of Topsannah. He declared: "You can tell Col. Homer Garrison that it was done with savvy fair as them Frenchmen would say" but "no body, just some East Texas sand and a legend" were sent by the Texans to fulfill the request from the Oklahoma Parkers. (Documents including a photocopy of a report of Redding's statement reproduced from the *Houston Chronicle*, October 3, 1965,

in the Quanah Papers, Archives of Fort Sill, Oklahoma)

54. A typescript in the Quanah Papers, Archives of Fort Sill, Oklahoma.

55. A letter reported to have been written by Quanah was circulated in Texas in which the Comanche chief pled for the right to bury his mother's remains. The statement began with the words "My mother. She fed me. She held me. She carried me . . ." and concluded with this plea: "Her dust, my dust, white brothers, your mother, you bury, My mother, I boy. Her dust, I bury. I sit on her mound. Love mother. Boy plead. My mother." (Jackson, *op. cit.* 127, 128) Contemporary records, however, indicate that the Parkers of Texas cooperated fully with Quanah's request to locate and remove the remains of Cynthia Ann to a site near his home in Oklahoma.

56. *The Lawton Daily News,* February 23, 1911.

57. Copy of a letter written by Quanah to "Col. Goodnight," dated January 7, 1911, in the Quanah Papers, Archives of Fort Sill, Oklahoma.

58. One account stated that Quanah's death occurred immediately after he had participated in a peyote meeting in Cheyenne County where he became very ill. (An interview with Knox Beal, Cache, Oklahoma, 1938, recorded in the Panhandle-Plains Historical Museum, Canyon, Texas)

59. A photostat of Quanah's death certificate is among the Quanah Papers, Archives of Fort Sill, Oklahoma.

60. A typescript in the Quanah Papers, Archives of Fort Sill, Oklahoma.

61. Letter of John D. Brister, July 14, 1958, in the Quanah Papers, Archives of Fort Sill, Oklahoma.

62. This statement was written by an army officer named Swett, probably the Morris Swett who was instrumental in bringing together many of the Parker documents into a collection in Fort Sill. The Swett memo is among the Quanah Papers in the Archives of Fort Sill, Oklahoma.

63. A typescript in the Quanah Papers, Archives of Fort Sill, Oklahoma.

64. J. Evetts Haley stated that the Quanah monument represented a "spear shaped dart pointing the way to heaven." (Haley, "Focus on the Frontier," *The Shamrock,* Spring 1957, 18)

65. All three monuments are clearly visible upon entering the small cemetery which is situated near the north central portion of the older section of Fort Sill.

XV. End of an Era

1. A statement made to the author in May 1986 by a Comanche living in Oklahoma who was a descendant of Quanah Parker.

2. Carter, *op. cit.*, 3.

3. *Ibid.*, 6.

4. Holland, *op. cit.*, 53.

XVI. The Ghosts of Blanco Canyon

1. Capt. R. G. Carter of the Fourth U.S. Cavalry, who participated in the 1871–1875 campaign against the Quohadi, later recalled that "we scouted out from the base of Soldier's Mound." (A typescript in the Quanah Papers, Panhandle-Plains Historical Museum, Canyon, Texas)

2. Haley, *Fort Concho and the Texas Frontier.* 186.

3. The Marfa Lights, ghostly illuminations which appear near Marfa, Texas, from time to time, represent another legend of apparitions of Indians of the past. There are those who claim these lights are the spirits of the Comanches who once roamed the area.

Appendix I: The Death of Nocona

1. DeShields, *op. cit.*, 50 ff.

2. Rupert Richardson, "The Death of Nocona and the Recovery of Cynthia Ann Parker," *Southwestern Historical Quarterly*, Volume 46, Number 1, 21.

3. Mayhall, *op. cit.*, 282.

4. Richardson, "The Death of Nocona," 46:21.

5. Corwin, *op. cit.*, 63.

6. A manuscript in the Quanah Papers, Panhandle-Plains Historical Museum, Canyon, Texas, with the following notation: "Dictated to J. Evetts Haley, Nov. 13, 1926 by Charles Goodnight."

7. Bill Neeley, *Quanah Parker and His People*, 62.

8. Richardson, "The Death of Nocona," 46:21.

9. The author discussed the question of the death of Nocona with descendants of Quanah Parker living in Cache, Oklahoma, in May 1986. They affirmed the family conviction which was based on statements from Quanah that Nocona was not killed in 1860 and that both Quanah and his father were in the Wichita Mountains at the time of the raid.

Appendix II: The Birth of Quanah

1. Charles Sommer, *op. cit.*, 16.

2. *Ibid.*, 46.

3. Richardson, "The Death of Nocona," Volume 46, footnote to page 15.

4. Neeley, *op. cit.*, 47.

5. Obituary notice from the *Lawton News*, February 28, 1911, a copy of which has been preserved among the Quanah Papers, Archives of Fort Sill, Oklahoma.

6. A typescript in the Dixon Papers, Panhandle-Plains Historical Museum, Canyon, Texas.

7. Neeley, *op. cit.*, 47.

8. Newcomb, *op. cit.*, 161.

9. Horr, *op. cit.*, 20.

10. A manuscript in the Quanah Papers, Archives of Fort Sill, Oklahoma.

Appendix III: The Literature of White Captives

1. E. House was the author of a work published in St. Louis in 1839 entitled *A Narrative of the Captivity of Mrs. Horn and her Two Children with that of Mrs. Harris by the Comanche* [sic] *Indians.*

2. A reprint of Babb's work was published in 1923.

3. Nystel's second edition of the record of his experiences was reprinted in 1930.

4. Nystel, *op. cit.*, 9–11.

5. Ben Moore's account related the fact that A. E. Butterfield, whose great uncle was John Butterfield of Butterfield Trail fame, was captured by Quanah during the final days of Indian warfare.

6. Wayne Gard, "The Mooar Brothers," *Southwestern Historical Quarterly*, Volume 63, Number 1.

Appendix IV: Comanche Religion and the Ghost Dance

1. Plummer, *op. cit.*, 13.

2. David E. Jones, *op. cit.*, 49.

3. Sanapia had learned her healing arts from her mother and believed herself to be "the last surviving Comanche Eagle Doctor."(*Ibid., ix, x*)

4. James Cosner interviewed a Comanche, Ethel B. Tackitt, in 1938

in which she spoke of ceremonial places and medicine mounds which had been determined by the religious practitioners of the tribe. (Interview notes in the Quanah Papers, Panhandle-Plains Historical Museum, Canyon, Texas)

5. A typescript of an interview with Anna Gomez by Ophelia D. Vestal in 1937 in Quanah Papers, Panhandle-Plains Historical Museum, Canyon, Texas.

6. An interview with Dick Banks in Marlow, Oklahoma, 1938, in the Quanah Papers, Panhandle-Plains Historical Museum, Canyon, Texas.

7. H. W. Baylor, *Frontier Times,* June 1929, 6:9.

8. A typescript of an interview with Anna Gomez in 1937 in the Quanah Papers, Panhandle-Plains Historical Museum, Canyon, Texas.

9. Plummer, *op. cit.,* 14.

10. Charles Sommer, *op. cit.,* 33.

11. A typescript containing a statement from Wayne Parker, a descendant of Quanah, in the Quanah Papers, Panhandle-Plains Historical Museum, Canyon, Texas.

12. Nystel, *op. cit.,* 9.

13. A typescript by Barbara Rila, Ph.D., "The Development of Religious Concepts."

14. A typescript in the Quanah Papers, Archives of Fort Sill, Oklahoma.

15. The ceremony of the Cedar Smoke was described to the author by a direct descendant of the Quohadi Comanches in an interview in May 1986.

16. *The Quanah Tribune-Chief: Centennial Edition,* Quanah, Texas, September 20, 1984.

17. An interview by the author with descendants of Quanah Parker living in Cache, Oklahoma, May 1986.

18. Hagan, *op. cit.,* 186.

19. Waldman, *op. cit.,* 153.

20. Wilcomb E. Washburn, *The Indian in America,* 222.

21. A manuscript letter dated February 28, 1907, from the Wormser Brothers of Laredo, Texas, in the Quanah Papers, Archives of Fort Sill, Oklahoma.

22. Wilcomb E. Washburn, *The American Indian and the United States: A Documentary History,* 4:2788.

23. Pate, *op. cit.,* 16.

24. *Ibid.,* 17.

25. Wissler, *op. cit.,* 125.

26. Dee Brown, *op. cit.,* 254.

27. A typescript in the Quanah Papers, Archives of Fort Sill, Oklahoma, which reported an account of the Adobe Walls battle which was related to Capt. Hugh Scott in 1897.

APPENDIX V: ORAL TRADITION AND THE SEARCH FOR FACTUAL DATA CONCERNING CYNTHIA ANN PARKER

1. The National Archives Microfilm Publication, Microcopy Number 606, Roll 13, ii.

Bibliography

Manuscripts and Documents
in the Texas State Archives
Austin, Texas

"Biographies of Leading Texans" [Typescript in the Texas State Ar-
chives, Austin, Texas], Volume 3.
Lamar Papers, Manuscript Numbers 164, 995, 1100, 1372, 1373, 1855,
1863, 1874, 1922, and 2166.
Wharton, C. R. *The Baron of Bastrop*. n.d. [A rare pamphlet in the Texas
State Archives, Austin, Texas.]

Papers and Materials in
Cache, Oklahoma

*Parker Scrapbook: a collection of papers, clippings, reproduced documents and related
memorabilia in the possession of Baldwin Parker, Jr., grandson of Quanah
Parker*. (This collection was made available to the author by Baldwin
Parker, Jr., in his home in Cache, Oklahoma, in May 1986.)
Wildlife Refuge Reservation Paper, a paper prepared for public information
and distributed at the Quanah Parker Center located in the Wildlife
Refuge Reservation near Cache, Oklahoma.

Manuscripts and Documents in
the Archives of Fort Sill, Oklahoma

Quanah Papers in the Archives of Fort Sill, Oklahoma. (A collection of
papers relating to Quanah Parker housed in the Archives Building of
Fort Sill. This includes manuscript letters attributed to Quanah, letters addressed to him, papers concerning his activities as a reserva-

tion chief, as well as a variety of other documents including records of interviews with Indians which represent tribal oral tradition concerning the final days of the Comanche nation.)

Papers and Manuscripts
in the Panhandle-Plains Historical Museum
Research Center, Canyon, Texas

A collection of papers relating to Quanah Parker which includes typescripts of interviews with descendants of Quanah and others who had known the Comanche chief, along with information regarding the culture of the South Plains Indians.

Papers in the Manuscript Department
University of North Carolina, Chapel Hill

References to Indian warfare on the frontier in the Battle Family Papers, the Armand Soubie Papers, and the Margaret Anne Ulmer Papers.

Documents in Washington, D.C.

Office of Indian Affairs. Manuscript letters and documents on microfilm representing the correspondence of the Office of Indian Affairs. The National Archives, Washington, D.C.

Parker, Daniel. Manuscript letter in the Manuscript Division of the Library of Congress, Box 186, 1821, Washington, D.C.

Articles, Printed Papers and Typescripts

Baylor, H. W. Frontier Times, Volume 6, Number 9 (June 1929)

Becker, Daniel A. "Comanche Civilization With a History of Quanah Parker." *Chronicles of Oklahoma.* Oklahoma Historical Society, 1921–1923, Volume I.

Bryant, Scarlett Kidd. *Under the Parker Tree.* (A paper privately published by descendants of Quanah Parker which included both documented sources and information from family members) Ada, Oklahoma: Ray James and Associates, Printers, 1970.

Buchanan, James. *Message From the President of the United States, Difficulties on the Southwestern Frontier.* 36th Congress, First Session, House of Representatives.

Carriker, Robert C., editor. "Thompson McFadden's Diary of An Indian Campaign," *Southwestern Historical Quarterly*, Volume 75, Number 2, (October 1971).

Christian, A. K. "Mirabeau B. Lamar," *Southwestern Historical Quarterly*, Volumes 23 and 24, 1922.

Clark, Fannie McAlpine. "A Chapter in the History of a Young Territory," *Texas Historical Association Quarterly*, Volume 9.

Fallwell, Gene. *The Comanche Trail of Thunder and the Massacre at Parker's Fort.* Historic Trails Society Bulletin, 1960.

Field, William T. "Review of *Comanche Land* by J. Emmon Harston," *Southwestern Historical Quarterly*, Volume 67, (October 1963).

Gard, Wayne. "The Mooar Brothers, Buffalo Hunters," *Southwestern Historical Quarterly*, Volume 63, Number 1, (July 1959).

Graham, Phillip. "Mirabeau Bounaparte Lamar's First Trip to Texas," *Southwest Review*, Volume 21, (July 1939).

Haley, J. Evetts. *Charles Goodnight's Indian Recollections.* Reprinted from the *Panhandle–Plains Historical Review*, 1928.

Haley, J. Evetts. "Focus on the Frontier," *The Shamrock*, Spring 1957.

Hessler, Samuel D. "Daniel Parker, 1781–1844 and the Establishment of The Pilgrim Church, 1833, the First Baptist Church in Texas." (Typescript)

House Document Number 76, Second Session, 29th Congress. Letter from P. M. Butler and M. G. Lewis, Indian Commissioners, to W. Medill, Commissioner of Indian Affairs, Washington City, D.C., August 8, 1846.

Mayhall, Mildred P. "Book Reviews: *Cynthia Ann Parker*, by Grace Jackson," *Southwestern Historical Quarterly*, Volume 64, Number 2, (October 1960).

Oliphant, Jo Ann. "Parker's Fort Deeply Etched in History," *Bi-Stone Review*, Mexia, Texas, 1977.

Pate, J'Nell. "The Battles of Adobe Walls," *Great Plains Journal*, Volume 16, Number 1 (Fall 1976).

Quanah Tribune–Chief, Centennial Edition. Quanah, Texas, September 20, 1984.

Richardson, Rupert N., editor. "The Death of Nocona and The Recovery of Cynthia Ann Parker," *Southwestern Historical Quarterly*, Volume 46, Number 1, (July 1942).

Rister, Carl C., editor. "Documents Relating to General W. T. Sherman's Southern Plains Indian Policy 1871–1875," *Panhandle–Plains Historical Review*, Number 9, (1936).

Townsend, David H. "The Enemy," *Southwest Heritage*, Summer 1974, pp. 29–33.

U.S. Bureau of Indian Affairs. *Texas Indians, 29th Congress, Second Session,*

Document Number 76, Report of W. L. Marcy, Secretary of War. Washington: United States Printing Office, n.d.

Williams, J. W. "The Van Dorn Trails." *Southwestern Historical Quarterly*, Volume 44, Number 3 (January 1941).

A Selected Bibliography of Books and Printed Works

Babb, T. A. *In the Bosom of the Comanches.* Dallas, Texas: Hargreaves Printing Company, Second Edition, 1923.

Barker, Eugene. *The University of Texas Record.* Austin, Texas, Volume II.

Barness, Larry. *Heads, Hides and Horns.* Fort Worth, Texas: Texas Christian University Press, 1985.

Benner, Judith Ann. *Sul Ross: Soldier, Statesman, Educator.* College Station: Texas A and M University Press, 1983.

Brinkley, William Campbell. *The Texas Revolution.* Baton Rouge: Louisiana State University Press, 1952.

Brown, Dee. *Bury My Heart at Wounded Knee: An Indian History of the American West.* New York: Bantam Books, 1970.

Brown, John Henry. *Comanche Raid of 1840.* Houston: Union National Bank, 1933.

Butterfield, A. E. *Comanche, Kiowa and Apache Missions: Forty-two Years Ago and Now. Interesting and Thrilling Incidents.* Childress, Texas, 1934.

Canales, Isidio Vizcaya. *La Invasion De Los Indios Barbaros Al Noreste De Mexico En Los Anos De 1840 y 1841.* Monterrey, 1968.

Capps, Benjamin. *The Old West: The Indians.* New York: Time-Life Books, 1973.

Carter, Robert Goldthwaite. *Tragedies of Canyon Blanco. Washington: Gibson Brothers, Printers, 1919.*

Cash, Joseph H., and Gerald W. Wolff. The Comanche People. Phoenix: Indian Tribal Series, 1974.

Castañeda, Carlos Eduardo. *The Mexican Side of the Texas Revolution.* Dallas: The Turner Company, 1928.

Clarke, Mary Whatley. *Chief Bowles and the Texas Cherokees.* Norman, Oklahoma: University of Oklahoma Press, 1971.

Conger, Robert N., et al. *Rangers of Texas.* Waco, Texas: Texian Press, 1969.

Connor, Seymour V. *Adventure in Glory.* Austin: Steck-Vaughn Company, 1965.

Copeland, Fayette. *Kendall of the Picayune.* Norman, Oklahoma: University of Oklahoma Press, 1963.

Corwin, Hugh D. *Comanche and Kiowa Captives.* Guthrie, Texas: Cooperative Publishers, 1959.

Day, Donald, and Harry Herberts Ullom, editors. *The Autobiography of Sam Houston*. Norman, Oklahoma: University of Oklahoma Press, 1954.

Day, James M., editor. *Senate Journal of the Ninth Legislature of the State of Texas, Regular Session, November 4, 1861–January 14, 1862*.

DeShields, James T. *Cynthia Ann Parker: The Story of Her Capture*. San Antonio: The Naylor Company, 1934. (This is a reprint of the original published for the author in St. Louis in 1886. Although the reprint appeared nearly half a century after the original work, an addition to the original preface indicates that the author was still living and gave sanction to the second edition.)

Dixon, Sam Houston, and Louis Wiltz Kemp. *The Heroes of San Jacinto*. Houston: The Anson Jones Press, 1932.

Dollbeare, Benjamin. *A Narrative of the Captivity and the Suffering of Dolly Webster Among the Camanche [sic] Indians of Texas*. New Haven: Yale University Library, 1986.

Douglas, C. L. *Gentlemen in White Hats*. Dallas: South-West Press, 1934.

Eastman, Edwin. *Seven and Nine Years Among the Camanches [sic] and Apaches*. Jersey City, N.J.: Published by Clark Johnson, 1874.

Edmunds, R. David, editor. *Studies in Diversity: American Indian Leaders*. Lincoln, Nebraska: University of Nebraska Press, 1980.

Falconer, Thomas. *Letters and Notes on the Texas Santa Fe Expedition, 1841–1842*. New York: Dauber and Price, 1930.

Fehrenbach, T. R. *Comanches: The Destruction of a People*. New York: Alfred A. Knopf, 1974.

———. *Lone Star: A History of Texas and the Texans*. New York: Macmillan Publishing Company, Inc.,1968.

Fern, Veroilius, editor. *An Encyclopedia of Religion*. New York: The Philosophical Library, 1945.

Foreman, Paul. *Quanah: The Serpent Eagle*. Flagstaff, Arizona: Northland Press, 1983.

Frost, John. *Thrilling Adventures Among the Indians*. Philadelphia: John E. Potter and Company, n.d.

Gallagher, Peter. *The Santa Fe Expedition*. Dallas, 1935.

Gilles, Albert S., Sr. *Comanche Days*. Dallas: SMU Press, 1974.

Gonzalez, Catherine Troxell. *Cynthia Ann Parker*. Austin, Texas: Eakin Press, 1980.

Hagan, William T. *United States-Comanche Relations: The Reservations Years*. New Haven: Yale University Press, 1976.

Haley, J. Evetts. *Fort Concho and the Texas Frontier*. San Angelo, Texas: San Angelo Standard-Times, 1952.

Harston, J. Emmor. *Comanche Land*. San Antonio: The Naylor Company, 1963.

Havins, Thomas Robert. *Beyond the Cimarron: Major Earl Van Dorn in Co-manche Land.* Brownwood, Texas: The Brown Press, 1968.

Held, John A. *Religion, A Factor in Building Texas.* San Antonio: The Naylor Company, 1940.

Hill, Edward E. *American Indians.* Washington: National Archives and Records Service, 1981.

Hofland, Barbara (Wreaks) Hoale. *The Stolen Boy: a Story Founded on Facts.* London: A. K. Newman and Company, n.d. [photocopy]

Hogan, W. R. *The Texas Republic: A Social and Economic History.* Austin: University of Texas Press, 1964.

Hohes, Pauline Buck. *Centennial History of Anderson County.* San Antonio: The Naylor Press, 1936.

Holden, William Curry. *A Ranching Saga: the Lives of William Elections Halsell and Ewing Halsell.* San Antonio: Trinity University Press, 1976.

Holland, G. A., assisted by Violet M. Roberts. *History of Parker County and the Double Log Cabin: Being a Brief Symposium of the Early History of Parker County, Together With Short Biographical Sketches of Early Settlers and Their Trials.* Weatherford, Texas: The Herald Publishing Company, 1937.

Horr, David Agee, editor. *Kiowa-Commanche* [sic] *Indian Transcripts of Hearings of the Kiowa, Commanche, and Apache Tribes of Indians vs. The United States of America. 2 volumes.* New York: Garland Publishing Company, Inc., 1974.

House, E. A Narrative of the Captivity of Mrs. Horn and her Two Children with that of Mrs. Harris by the Camanche [sic] *Indians.* St. Louis: C. Keemle, Printer, 1839.

Hunter, J. Marvin. *The Boy Captives.* Bandera, Texas: The Frontier Times, 1927.

Hyde, George E. *Rangers and Regulars.* Columbus, Ohio: Long's College Book Store, 1952. (This work was published in a limited edition.)

Jackson, Clyde L., and Grace Jackson. *Quanah Parker: Last Chief of the Comanches.* New York: Exposition Press, 1963.

Jackson, Grace. *Cynthia Ann Parker.* San Antonio: The Naylor Press, 1959.

James, Marquis. *The Raven.* New York: Blue Ribbon Books, Inc., 1929.

James, Vinton Lee. *Frontier and Pioneer Recollections of Early Days in San Antonio and West Texas.* San Antonio, Texas: Artes Graficas Press, 1938.

Jenkins, John Holland. Edited by John Holmes Jenkins, III. *Recollections of Early Texas.* Austin: University of Texas Press, 1958.

Johnson, Frank W. *A History of Texas and Texans.* Chicago: American Historical Society, 1914.

Jones, David E. *Sanapia: Comanche Medicine Woman.* New York: Holt, Rinehart and Winston, 1968.

Jones, Jonathan H. *A Condensed History of the Comanche and Apache Tribes.*

New York: Garland Publishing Company, 1976.

Kendall, George. *Narrative of the Texas Santa Fe Expedition*. 2 volumes. New York: Harper and Brothers, 1844.

Klotzbach, Kurt. *Der Adler der Comanchen: Quanah Parker*. Gottingen: W. Fischer-Verlag, 1976.

Lee, Nelson. *Three Years Among the Comanches*. Norman, Oklahoma: University of Oklahoma Press [a republication], 1957.

Lee, Nelson. *Three Years Among the Camanches* [sic], *the Narrative of Nelson Lee, the Texas Ranger*. Albany, New York: Baker Taylor, 1859 [photocopy].

Lehmann, Herman. *Nine Years Among the Indians, 1870–1879*. Austin: Von Boeckmann-Jones Company, 1927.

Loftin, Jack. *Trails Through Archer*. Burnet, Texas: Nortex Press, 1979.

McLean, Malcolm. *Papers Concerning Robertson's Colony in Texas*. Volume X. Arlington, Texas: The University of Texas at Arlington Press, 1983.

Marcy R. B. Edited and annotated by Grant Foreman. *Adventures on the Red River*. Norman: University of Oklahoma, 1937. (The first printing of this work was dated 1853.)

———. *Exploration of the Red River of La. in the year 1852*. Washington: A. O. P. Nicholson, Public Printer, 1854.

———. *The Prairie Traveler, A Hand-book for Overland Expeditions*. New York: Harper and Brothers, Publishers, 1859. (Reproduced in 1981 by Time-Life Books.)

———. *Thirty Years of Army Life on the Border*. New York: Harper and Brothers, 1866.

Mayhall, Mildred P. *Indian Wars of Texas*. Waco, Texas: Texian Press, 1965.

Moore, Ben, Sr. *Seven Years with the Wild Indians*. O'Donnell, Texas, 1945.

Morrison, Samuel Elliot, and Henry Steele Commager. *The Growth of the American Republic*. New York: Oxford University Press, 1942.

Neeley, Bill. *Quanah Parker and His People*. Slaton, Texas: The Brazos Press, 1986.

Nevins, David. *The Old West: The Soldiers*. New York: Time-Life Books, 1973.

Newcomb, W. W., Jr. *The Indians of Texas: From Prehistoric to Modern Times*. Austin: University of Texas Press, 1969.

Newell, Chester. *History of the Revolution in Texas*. New York: Wiley and Putnam, 1838. Reprinted by the Steck Company of Austin, 1935.

Newton, Lewis, and Herbert Gambrell. *A Social and Political History of Texas*. Dallas: The Turner Company, 1935.

Nye, W. S. *Carbine and Lance*. Norman: University of Oklahoma Press, 1937.

Nystel, Ole T. *Lost and Found or Three Months with the Wild Indians.* Dallas, Texas: Williams Brothers, 1888.

————. *From Bondage to Freedom or Three Months with the Wild Indians.* (A second edition of Nystel's *Lost and Found or Three Months with the Wild Indians.*) Keene, Texas: The College Press, 1930.

Parker, James W. *The Rachel Plummer Narrative.* Published by Rachel Lofton, Susie Hendricks, and Jane Kennedy, 1926.

Parker, W. B. *Notes Taken During the Expedition Commanded by Captain R. B. Marcy, USA, Through Unexplored Texas in the Summer and Fall of 1854.* Austin: Texas State Historical Association, 1984. (A reprint of the original published in 1856.)

Place, Marian T. *Comanches and Other Indians of Texas.* New York: Harcourt, Brace and World, 1970.

Plummer, Rachel. *Rachel Plummer's Narrative.* Preface by Archibald Hanna and an introduction by William S. Reese (A photographic reproduction of the only known copy of the original work printed in 1838.) Austin: Republished by the Jenkins Company, 1977.

————. *Narrative of the Capture and Subsequent Sufferings of Mrs. Rachel Plummer.* (A republication.) Waco: Texian Press, 1968.

Plummer, Zula. *The Search for Rachel,* [No publisher listed], 1976.

Pratt, William. *Galveston Island.* Austin: University of Texas Press, 1954.

Raht, Carlysle Graham. *The Romance of Davis Mountains and Big Bend Country* [Edition Texana]. Odessa, Texas: The Rahtbooks Company, 1963.

Richardson, Rupert N. *The Comanche Barrier to the South Plains Settlement.* Glendale, California: The Arthur H. Clark Company, 1933.

Rister, Carl Coke. *Border Captives.* Norman, Oklahoma: University of Oklahoma Press, 1940.

Smith, Coho. *Cohographs.* Fort Worth: Blanch-Smith, 1976.

Sommer, Charles H. *Quanah Parker: Last Chief of the Comanches.* Printed by the Quanah, Acme and Pacific Railway, 1945.

Sommer, Jeanne. *Comanche Revenge.* Wayne, Pennsylvania: The Dell Publishing Company, 1981.

Sowell, A. J. *Rangers and Pioneers of Texas.* New York: Sentry Press, 1964 [a reprint of the original published in 1884].

Steen, Ralph W. *History of Texas.* Austin: The Steck Company, 1939.

Sweet, William Warren. *The Story of Religion in America.* New York: Harper Brothers, 1930.

Taylor, Joe F., compiler. *The Indian Campaign on the Staked Plains, 1874-1875: Military Correspondence From War Department Adjutant General's Office, File 2815 — 1874.* Canyon, Texas: The Panhandle-Plains Historical Society, 1962.

Tilghman, Zoe A. *Quanah: The Eagle of the Comanches.* Oklahoma City, Oklahoma: Harlow Publishing Corporation, 1938.

Tinkle, Lon. *Thirteen Days to Glory.* New York: McGraw-Hill, 1985.

Tolbert, Frank. *The Day of San Jacinto.* New York: McGraw-Hill, 1959.

Utley, Robert M. *The Indian Frontier of the American West 1846–1890.* Albuquerque: University of New Mexico Press, 1984.

Waldman, Carl. *Atlas of the North American Indian* [with maps and illustrations by Molly Braun]. New York: Facts on File Publications, 1985.

Waldraven-Johnson, Margaret. *The White Comanche: The Story of Cynthia Ann Parker and her Son, Quanah.* New York: Comet Press Books, 1956.

Wallace, Ernest, and E. Adamson Hoebel. *The Comanches: Lords of the South Plains.* Norman, Oklahoma: University of Oklahoma Press, 1952.

Walter, Ray A. *A History of Limestone Country.* Austin, Texas: Von Boeckmann-Jones, 1959.

Washburn, Wilcomb E. *The American Indian and the United States: A Documentary History.* 4 volumes. New York: Random House, 1973.

———. *The Indian in America.* New York: Harper and Row, Publishers, 1975.

Webb, Walter Prescott. *The Story of the Texas Rangers.* Austin: Encino Press, Second Edition, 1971.

Weems, John Edward. *Death Song: The Last of the Indian Wars.* New York: Doubleday and Company, Inc., 1976.

Wilbarger, J. W. *Indian Depredations in Texas.* Volume one in the Brasada Reprint Series, Austin: The Pemberton Press, 1967. (A reprint of a work originally published c. 1889.)

Wilson, Jane Adeline. *A Thrilling Narrative of the Sufferings of Mrs. Jane Adeline Wilson During Her Captivity Among the Comanche Indians.* Fairfield, Washington: Ye Galleon Press, 1971. (The 1971 printing was a limited edition of the original work published in 1854, soon after Jane Wilson's rescue from the Comanches. Her story was first printed in the *Weekly Gazette* of Santa Fe, New Mexico, on December 24, 1853.)

Wissler, Clark. *Indians of the Plains.* Lancaster, Pennsylvania: Lancaster Press, 1927.

Quanah Parker in his home at Fort Sill, Oklahoma. Nearby is a potrait of his mother, Cythia Ann Parker, holding her young daughter, Prairie Flower.
— Courtesy Smithsonian Institution National Anthropological Archives, Bureau of American Ethnology Collection

Quanah Parker's home at Cache, near Fort Sill, Oklahoma, a large frame dwelling with outbuildings enclosed by a picket fence. Circa 1892.
— Courtesy Smithsonian Institution National Anthropological Archives, Bureau of American Ethnology Collection

Quanah Parker, the last chief of the Comanches, on horseback in full ceremonial battle dress at Lawton, Oklahoma.

Quanah Parker, last chief of the Comanches, is shown here with five other Indian leaders. The portrait was taken in 1905 at Carlisle, Pennsylvania, prior to a trip to Washington, D.C., where the group headed the Carlisle Indian students in the inaugural parade of Theodore Roosevelt. Shown are Little Plume, Blackfoot; Buckskin Charlie, Ute; Geronimo, Apache; Quanah Parker; Hollow Horn Bear, Dakota; and American Horse, Dakota.

Quanah Parker dressed in the "white man's clothing."
— Courtesy Western History Collections, University of Oklahoma Library

Children of Quanah Parker and grandchildren of Cynthia Ann, 1891–1893.
— Courtesy Smithsonian Institution National Anthropological Archives,
Bureau of American Ethnology Collection

Index

175

CPSIA information can be obtained
at www.ICGtesting.com
Printed in the USA
BVHW051601310721
612915BV00007B/984